REAL LIFE - REAL PAIN - REAL LOVE

REAL LIFE - REAL PAIN - REAL LOVE

Insights Into Therapy and Transference from a Patient's Perspective

Judy Sullivan

ISBN-13: 978-1500688-73

ISBN-10:150068807X

DEDICATION

To Doug: For being perfect. Perfect for me. For teaching me, listening to me, accepting me, and in your own way, I think, caring for me. You didn't give up on me, so I didn't give up on myself. Without you, my life might have spiraled out of control. Thank you for making sure it didn't. I hope you enjoy this book. It was written especially for you...and me.

CONTENTS

ACKNOWLEDGMENTS

A special thank you to Betty for listening to me without judgment and for being my friend through "thick and thin". Thank you to Elizabeth for helping me work through the grief. And to Lynn for encouraging me to write and express my feelings. And to Pat for her help in navigating the road to publishing this first book. I couldn't have completed this very special project without all of you. You had confidence in me, which in turn helped me have confidence in myself. Thank you sincerely.

FORWARD

One thing I know for sure. No amount of "textbook learning" can adequately convey the impact a counselor/therapist has on a client's life. This book, based on a real patient's experiences, delves deeply into the psyche of a client and attempts through essays, letters and poems to express the deep, intimate emotions a client feels during a strong "therapeutic alliance" and forced "termination".

Like a thought-provoking novel, these writings show the wide range and depth of feelings elicited through deeply intimate emotional exchanges over an 8 year period. When the author receives word her much loved and respected therapist will be leaving in a year and moving out of state, her world is shattered as her life begins to spiral out of control. When he does indeed depart, the grieving begins in earnest, as she is catapulted into the final stages of the therapeutic process.

A must read for future therapists, counselors and those who educate those future counselors, as well as anyone who has ever been in therapy or is considering it. As Maya Angelou said "When You Know Better, You Will Do Better". In that context, when a therapist, future therapist, graduate student or a therapist in training can fully comprehend how deeply they can influence a client's life, they hopefully will be able to understand and be more empathetic to those fragile clients they may counsel in the future.

To quote Taylor Caldwell, "The most desperate need of men today is not a new vaccine for any disease, or a new religion, or a new 'way of life' ...his real need, his most terrible need, is for someone to listen to him, not as a 'patient' but as a human soul." My fervent hope is that this book, gut wrenching as it was to write and to experience, will be worthwhile if only one person realizes they need not suffer in silence... if only one person realizes they are not alone.

BACKGROUND

Though it may not seem so from some of these writings, I am generally a happy person. I have a great sense of humor. I am involved in so many volunteer activities, I have to keep 3 calendars. I have many interests; sometimes it's hard to focus on just one. I feel I **need** to be busy all the time. I like people. I'm empathetic. I'm caring. You would probably like me. Most people do. Unfortunately, most of my problems over the years have been because of my lack of self esteem. Most of my poor decisions were made from lack of self confidence. In the past, I haven't liked myself very much.

I was a shy, chubby child and teen. I absolutely despised having my picture taken from as young as 3 years old. Still do. That would explain why I threw out all the pictures from my childhood and beyond several years ago. My clothes came from the Spiegel's catalog. I had permanents in my hair and wore saddle shoes in high school. I've come a long way, but I've never shed that image of the quiet, shy, awkward, ugly young girl. I see her so clearly. She is me.

From a young age, at stressful times, I would chew on my hair, bite my fingernails, rub on my eyebrows until they were gone …and worse. I hated doing it, but I couldn't stop. Some behaviors I still can't control, for example the nail biting. Embarrassed, I suffered in silence. Now I have learned that these actions were some of my earliest impulse control problems, and they often occur with other psychiatric disorders, including anxiety (GAD), OCD, ADD and Depression.

I think I always tried to be perfect…get good grades, be the good kid, be the perfect daughter, be the person teachers and those in authority liked, the person people could depend on. I felt so inferior because of my lack of social skills coupled with never being pretty like my sister, or thin or popular, yet I had and have such high (often unachievable) expectations for myself and others. Looking back, a lot of my life choices were made because I didn't want to disappoint or fail.

I am extremely sensitive to criticism, and when I receive it, I can't bounce back. I can't say "So what?" or "Who cares?" or "That's just your opinion". Instead I obsess for days over the most minute critical remark. When this happens, often my first reaction is "I wish I were dead". As long as I can remember, I have suffered from non-stop worries and anxieties, coupled with low self esteem and insecurity about people's intentions. I often see events in negative, intimidating and critical ways. I know the reactions are excessive, troubling, hard to control; they've been a problem seemingly forever.

Criticism may not even be directed at me, but I'm going to process it internally, ruminate and become anxious. I hate that about myself. I react and my emotions change quickly. Minor changes "throw me for a loop". I lose focus and forget what I'm doing, or what I should be doing, and jump immediately to something else, never completing what I've started. I want instant gratification. When I want something, I want it NOW. My head is always filled with thoughts. Some of them are sad and some of them are happy; some are rational, some are not. I'm often frustrated by my inability to better control my thoughts and emotions. I'm much improved now compared to how I used to be. I don't handle disappointment well. I often blow things out of proportion and then obsess about them.

I crave affection. I fantasize (though believe me, fantasies about D are making for an "interesting" book that will be coming out soon). I think of regrets about things I could have done better. People I didn't treat as well as I could have. Situations I should have handled differently.

In the past, I often thought it would have been better if I hadn't been born, as it is so hard to lose people you love and to know you are going to die also. I often feel I haven't made any contributions to other peoples' lives - that I haven't made any impact on the world at large - that the good times haven't outweighed the bad. If I hadn't been born, it wouldn't have made any real difference one way or the other. Other times, I put it in perspective, and admit a lot of people do like me. I do make a difference. I am compassionate and a good friend. I worked at a toxic job that tore me down and pulled me apart. Retirement meant I could pursue my passion for writing and gardening and volunteering. I am at peace when doing those pleasurable activities. Of course, playing with my grandkids is the greatest fun.

It's a special treat looking out my office window and seeing my garden, the bright sun, and the fields, filled with hay bales, stretched out in front of me during the summer. And the snowmobilers racing past in the winter. Deer, rabbits, an occasional turkey, and young foxes are all visible from the house.

I'm healthy. I'm active…alert…alive. Even with the "bumps in the road" along the way, life is pretty darn good. I've been in the depths of despair…contemplated suicide several times when things were overwhelming at work and life was out of control. But you know what? I didn't do it. I had great friends, great support, a wonderful Nurse Practitioner, who was my kind and loving friend and confidant, and of course D, who scheduled appointments every week during the "dark times."

It's very important to me that every patient who can identify with these feelings knows that it does get better. Therapy often progresses 2 steps forward, 1 step back…BUT it does progress. Problems ebb and flow but they get worked through and often disappear. They certainly lessen.

11

The important thing is your Therapist is there for you. That you trust him/her. That you open up and share…everything. It's okay - they will understand. Nothing shocks them. They've pretty much heard it all. Imagine having someone you can trust absolutely and completely. Someone who has boundaries and will never cross them, for your safety and protection. Someone who has no hidden agenda. It's all about you. It's your dime…your time. The most important thing is they will travel along the road to healing right by your side. You aren't alone. You are going to be just fine. Please believe me.

Note to future therapists: Make sure you take care of these people you meet along the way. They need you. We need you. Read the book. Maybe just one sentence will jump out at you and you will be able to see yourself or relate it to one of your clients or see one of your clients in the description. And at that moment, hopefully you will understand just a little better how important you are, how important therapy is, to this hurting individual. Give them an emotional hug and don't ever forget them. We are all just human beings doing our best in this world at our own level of consciousness. Thank you for being there for us.

BEHAVIORAL THERAPY

Millions of people attend therapy sessions of one kind or another. I was and am one of those millions. People come for a variety of reasons, but usually because they are looking for help in areas of their lives they are unable to handle alone. The reasons why they enter therapy run the gamut from anxiety to impulse control problems to marital and/or family discord, as well as many other issues. Everybody is, I believe, different but the same. What most of us have in common is the need for an experienced counselor, in a totally non-critical way, to listen and give us feedback with which to handle the multitude of problems in our day-to-day lives. It sounds simple, but so many forces and attitudes are at play, many of them involving "family of origin", that it may start with one topic, but evolve into many others. Much has been written about these short term and long term psychological problems, yet every person is unique, making each problem and it's solution also the same, yet different.

There is still a prevalent attitude among a large percentage of the general public that there must be something wrong with a person in counseling. They must be "crazy" if they aren't able to handle their own problems. Just "suck it up" we hear or "You're going to a Shrink? What's wrong with YOU?" in that all too familiar superior tone of voice. So mental health becomes a forbidden topic, only shared with a few close friends and confidants.

What the general public may not be aware of, is the difference counseling in the form of therapy, in particular cognitive behavioral therapy, can make in an individual's life. Can you imagine what it would be like to have 50 minutes of "ME" time - where a person listens attentively to just YOU - never criticizing, always offering a calm and soothing presence, as well as good advice. They help you realize it is possible to feel better and get beyond whatever issue or issues you may, at this time, feel are disrupting your life and causing a myriad of physical and/or psychological symptoms. What could be better, right? It's a necessity that feels like a luxury, just like a trip to a Spa. Just relax and breathe. The session will usually leave you relaxed, calmer, happier and feeling better. If not those particular emotions, then you should at least feel more in control of your life than when you entered the office.

There are all types of therapists. They have years and years of intensive training in dealing with your problem(s). They have the education and training to personalize each session to benefit just you. Some people may have trouble expressing their feelings and emotions, but counselors know the leading questions to ask to make you at ease and able to share your deepest innermost thoughts and concerns. Yes, that does include the one that is always asked on TV programs, movies and in cartoons - "How does that make you feel?" Who else ever asks you that? And uses that information to help you understand why you feel the way you do. I suspect very few people would ask and fewer would care about your answer. They are too busy with their own lives. Not so the counselor. He/she has no hidden personal agenda except to help you. As I said before your dime, your time.

As the therapy progresses, it becomes more and more interesting as it evolves into examining your life experiences. You will learn things about yourself that you may never have considered during your lifetime. They actually might explain your past, and often your present, circumstances. Why you do what you do, what other behaviors may actually be intertwined with those for which you originally began seeing your therapist and in general terms, just how interesting the workings of the mind can be. Not to mention how our upbringing, our childhood experiences and unfortunately sometimes our traumas, impact us many years down the road - sometimes for our entire lives. Whatever questions you have, whatever feelings you do or don't have, your counselor will help you delve into them, while helping you understand and prepare yourself for future "trigger" situations.

Of course, there is one "downside" which often may begin to intrude during your therapy sessions, through no fault of the counselor, but because we are human beings and are all needy in one way or the other. I am speaking of "Transference". Unless you have taken psychology courses in college, you may never have heard this term. After you have experienced it, you will never be the same again.

Transference is defined as "transferring expectations, based on important relationships, to new individuals that we meet". In a "therapeutic alliance" basically the therapist becomes whoever or whatever is "missing" from a client's life (example: a parent or a spouse). The therapist becomes all those things and more.

Unless the subject comes up early in your therapy and is explained and discussed in detail with your counselor, when you begin to develop strong feelings for your therapist, you won't understand those feelings or know coping strategies to use while experiencing them. Most importantly, you must understand these intense feelings are natural and normal, and in fact are expected and necessary, in the "intimacy" of deeply personal therapy sessions.

Because a client's psyche is fragile, fantasizing that this person actually cares about your feelings and emotions, therefore "cares" about you personally, causes one to develop strong feelings of attachment similar to love, which progress to a point where you may believe there must be something "wrong" with you. You must be crazy, perverted or a freak. There must be something wrong, because you are lusting after a professional you see on a regular basis, but only in the confines of an office setting. You can rationalize the obvious. This is just a doctor who treats you and countless others with similar problems. These intrusive thoughts may escalate until nearly every waking hour involves fantasizing about this most amazing person, who is now such an integral part of your life.

Often your own marital situation may suffer, as this new "relationship" makes your own marriage appear lackluster and insignificant. No one can compare to your therapist. He's perfect - has no flaws - is the person you have always wanted to be with; therefore, your own spouse or significant other may pale in comparison. You begin thinking "look what I settled for" as you yearn for this unattainable God-like person. This dissatisfaction with reality, coupled with these feelings of "love" and "lust", may thrust a client into an unexpected emotional, albeit one -sided, affair with this perfect person. Though not a prerequisite, if he/she is (at least in your eyes) drop dead gorgeous, it may even evolve into sexual fantasies.

Were it not for the intensity of these emotions, one would never consider stalking, researching the Internet, secretly taping appointments to hear his/her voice, or attending meetings or functions where he or she will be present. Always remember, you are not a bad person, nor a freak or a pervert, nor would you act inappropriately on these feelings. This person is only a substitute for the time being for what is missing in your life - your unmet needs.

Transference is hard, really hard to work through. But once you confront the problem, develop the courage to share your feelings with your professional, and research of the subject shows you are "normal" - indeed many others have the same thoughts and emotionally charged feelings - then you begin to see a "light at the end of the tunnel".

Finding yourself in the same situation, don't give it. If you are lucky enough to have a good, really good, therapist, he or she will make you comfortable sharing these feelings, and together you will work towards replacing these inappropriate feelings with more acceptable ones. He or she has earned your respect and admiration. Your trust has never been broken. Just knowing your feelings have been validated lessen them, thus allowing you to expand and grow in other areas. If you falter, and you will, just know he or she will be there. The responsibility for your mental health is in excellent hands!

THE BEGINNING OF LOSS

Grieving the loss of my therapist began in October 2012, a year before our final appointment. Giving this much advance notice was supposed to prepare a client for the loss and allow time to work on problems yet to be solved in therapy. In theory this sounds like an acceptable goal, one both client and therapist can live with.

But the above "good termination" did not go exactly as planned. During the nearly 2 years since the letter came from the counseling center that D was leaving, my emotions have run the gamut. Unfortunately, they have not lessened to this day.

It was not just accepting the loss of a much loved and respected therapist, but it was the loss of a very special relationship, with someone I loved, idolized and idealized. I don't just miss D, I miss the special rapport - the special friendship - the special connection - when I was with him. My one salvation has been my writing. In the following chapters I have attempted to convey the deeply intense and personal emotions I have felt, those that I expressed to D and those I haven't shared until this time. These include feelings that I have lived with over the past 8 years, and new ones that came about after D's departure, ones I am still attempting to work through with a grief counselor. It's not over yet. It has not been easy. It has been said time heals all things. Eventually it will get better, I'm sure, but it will never be the same. I will never forget this extraordinary man, and the lessons learned during our time together those many years.

It might be hard to believe this is written by a 64 year old mother of 4 and grandmother of 8 beautiful grandchildren. Transference in all it's forms - idealizing, idolizing, erotic - can impact any age, any gender, any socioeconomic group. Most practitioners believe there cannot be a true therapeutic alliance unless a client does indeed form these deep, personal attachments to his or her counselor. It is believed the client must live with the frustration - the tension - of the relationship to be able to work out and solve his or her problems. I expect for a counselor with strict boundaries this is easy. Not so for the clients who live with this frustration daily, as well as the emotions associated with it.

It began nearly eight years earlier, in a nondescript white building down a long blacktopped driveway surrounded by plush green fields, an idyllic setting, in Upstate New York. The moment we met - even the first few appointments we had together - were less than memorable apparently. The ensuing seven years were not.

I'd gone to him on a doctor's referral. The doctor knew him personally, insisting I needed to see him - NOW. I'd rejected the suggestion many times over the preceding years, but this time was different. "I don't know why I need to go, but all right, I will", I remembered thinking. The sadness over the loss of my Dad, coupled with the less than loving relationship with my children at that time, finally caused me to acquiesce. Once the decision was made, then came the difficult part. I had to plead with him to see me. He wasn't taking on new patients. I guess I must have been persuasive or pathetic, or maybe he could ascertain from the desperate tone, the garbled speech, jumbled words and agitated demeanor that I did, indeed, need him - NOW. Mindless as I am, I can remember nothing from that initial appointment. He must have extended his hand and introduced himself. "Hello - I'm Doug S". It was the only appointment we'd have at that location, and the only time he would ever touch me until that final goodbye. Our boundaries were established immediately.

The years passed quickly - too quickly. He was there through my parents' deaths, 3 weddings, the births of 6 grandchildren, innumerable crises both at work and at home. He was there through family dysfunction, toxic work situations, operations and broken

19

bones, family illnesses, miscarriages, estrangements and a near suicide He was there - really there - for every high and low, every up and down for seven years of my life.

We had a good relationship, D and I. There was an easy give and take. I'm sure I was an "easy read". I was classic textbook - GAD plus a side of other "crazies", which I'm certain he recognized long before I did. I'm sure he knew many things about me I didn't know. He never had to "draw" anything out of me. One blogger commented to her therapist how incredibly well he understood her, and he replied it was because she had shown him. It was the same with D. There were no secrets, no subject off limits, nothing I couldn't share. It was empowering just knowing that.

I often tried to explain how it felt to be me. Here is one explanation.

It's not easy being me. It's really hard when there's no focus - too many directions - lack of control - emotions so close to the surface. It's not much fun to be sad so much and know it's your own mind working against you. If it's a chemical imbalance, please Somebody, give me something to put the chemicals back in balance. I feel fragmented...restless...in limbo...disconnected like I don't belong anywhere - not at home, not at work. I wake up early and go to bed late. I hate feeling like a prisoner of my own mind. I hate living in a mindless world...not being able to remember...to pay attention...and worse yet, always caring till it hurts. Nobody thinks the fat girl has feelings cause she's so jolly on the outside. No concentration... bouncing from project to project... thought to thought...never being able to relax...never listening (that really drives me crazy)...things to be done...gotta do them, gotta do them NOW.

As much as a physical disease, as much as a herniated disc or a broken arm, having a mind that is broken causes real pain. It causes tears, heartache, loneliness, despair and suffering. It's so mentally and physically exhausting, it drains one's body, one's mind and one's soul.

Can you imagine for a moment going into a manic mode? You're so wound up, like a spring wound tightly and then released. Or the bodybuilder at the Fair that slams the platform with a sledgehammer and the ball soars skywards. The harder it's hit, the higher it goes. But just as quickly as it reaches the top, it drops - quickly hitting rock bottom. Welcome to my Life. Think of a hamster on a treadmill running round and round in the wheel, faster and faster, heart beating a mile a minute. It feels so good ...until it doesn't.

And you know what? It's really lonely being me. It's being alone with my thoughts...introspective so much of the time. Nobody knows how I feel. It's like having an enemy inside me ...I'm never alone - the thoughts are always there. They have become my Demons. Yet the outside world would never guess. They all think I'm just a fun loving, outgoing free spirit. I wish. (Sometimes I am though and that helps my self esteem temporarily at least).

The only point we really disagreed on was my "researching" his personal life. With the Internet, it was easy. Who knew a person could find out, for example, all these facts on one website:

Plays sports
Enjoys hiking and camping
Enjoys the outdoors
Loves to travel
Likes music
Loves reading
Reads about world news & politics
Has children

Has elderly parents
Cares about healthy living
Enjoys gardening
Researches investments
Collects antiques
Is self-driven
Donates to causes
Donates to religious causes
Buys from Internet
Enjoys shopping
Buys health and beauty merchandise

I was obsessed with finding out what "made him tick", what made him the phenomenal person he is. I guess psychologically it might be said I wanted to be close to him; I wanted a connection. Hopefully the following paragraphs will help explain exactly why this was so important to me. I hope if D should read this, he will understand too.

You always wondered why I researched you. Of course, it was foremost an obsession - a compulsion - but here's another explanation, which given the time to think it through, most perfectly described my intentions.

Say you really admired a professor. You respected his judgment and accomplishments, his way of thinking, his ability to bring out the best in you - maybe he even saw something in you that you didn't understand or recognize about yourself. He was your mentor and he was your guide. He was famous and he chose to give you his time and attention to help you succeed. Might you not (in this media age where all is available if you know where to look) check him out, his qualifications and accomplishments? Wouldn't you be happy for him when he received awards, kudos, compliments? You wouldn't be doing anything wrong, ethically or morally. You wouldn't use the information to hurt, ridicule or defame him. Researching him and then collecting this information wasn't to be mean or disrespectful - just the opposite in fact. The information you discern leaves you confident in your opinion of the professor. You are even more determined to work towards the goals he suggests for you. His life, upbringing, education, extracurricular activities... they all have made him the person you so admire. He is a good man - someone you would be proud to call a friend - a perfect example of what is possible if you pursue your dreams. His passion inspires you to "set the world on fire".

*George Weinberg writes in "The Heart of Psychotherapy" that "if there is any reason for us to talk about ourselves, I think revealing a weakness is the best one. Often we can gain a person's confidence this way and help him see that even if he doesn't share our failing, he can do well in spite of some other failing of his. If he tends to idealize us, sometimes we can help him by showing a weakness...an important way we can make the ending easier for the patient is by talking about ourselves. In many cases, our very secrecy about our private life has created it's own mystique...if we talk about ourselves more, giving him some carefully chosen facts that we withheld for the sake of the transference, we start to reduce this magical hold on the patient...as we become specific individuals to him, the mystique dissipates. Leaving seems more feasible...Especially in that last session, **we should not hold back delight in his/her achievements... Often I tell the person that I would be eager to hear from them, a phone call, or a brief note letting me know how things are going. And of course if they want to schedule some further sessions, I will be available...those same people might want to consult with me years later...when the person does come in, it's because they choose to do so. It feels different to them. They have a sense that the therapy is over. Some do this as a way of reconfirming our presence. Then they're gone for good, knowing that we are available, but knowing, too, that they can do quite well without us.**"*

How I wish that D's beliefs were the same as Mr. Weinberg's…how I wish he would have "delighted in my achievements" (if there were any) and been "eager" to hear from me or have allowed a "consultation… to reconfirm his presence".

THE 5 STAGES OF GRIEF

I think I was most surprised - baffled even- before he left, at the new intense emotions I was experiencing. It is believed there are five (5) stages of grief. They include Denial, Anger, Bargaining, Depression and Acceptance.

Stage 1 - Denial

The entire pre-termination period (and far beyond), I was in denial. He could not possibly be leaving. As long as I kept seeing him on my regular twice monthly schedule, nothing could possibly be changing. It was hard to continue this self deception when (1) the For Sale sign went up in front of his home and (2) his N.Y. license plates were changed to New Hampshire ones. But still, I pushed the truth from my mind and rarely spoke about his imminent departure, except when reading him passages from The Book. Even then it was the main character - the "hero" - who was moving on...not D. This wasn't going to happen. If I begged and cajoled him enough, I was certain he wouldn't be able to walk away...abandoning all of us.

Stage 2 - Anger

Never had I felt anger towards this man. I didn't think you could be angry at a person you loved. I was wrong. I read on Grief.com "that the anger is just another indication of the intensity of your love. The anger becomes a bridge over the open sea, a connection from you to them. It is something to hold onto; and a connection made from the strength of anger feels better than nothing at all." So true.

It began in the late Spring of 2012, while reading numerous psychology books, I realized that everything I said, everything I did, everything I experienced was "typical". I wasn't unique. I wasn't special. It was there in black and white on the pages of all those books about psychotherapy. I was pissed. So I sat down at my computer, angry and disillusioned with the entire profession (including D), and wrote the following two essays. According to all the blogs, books etc. I read, we all want to be "special". It angered me that I was not; that I was just one of many. I was a Nobody Special. That after the 50 minutes was up, I didn't matter (or so I suspected).

I am experiencing the 2nd stage of Grief apparently - the anger. And the more I think about it, the angrier, or maybe just the more disgusted, I feel with myself ...and You.

I realize I feel degraded and disgusted with myself. I have opened myself foolishly to expressing my sadness and feelings about you. This scenario was set in place and escalated, and I am the only one who has been hurt. And I'm the fragile, mentally ill one in this alliance. Everything I've said and done can be found word for word, I'm sure, on the pages of textbooks and training manuals. I'm not a person obviously with unique problems. Everything is written in these books. I've read them. It had to have been, for you, just like listening to a college lecture on What to Expect from Patients Undergoing Psychotherapy. You probably have a script - for this emotion, do this and say that. And don't forget to nod your head and look concerned like you've never heard it before. If my mind is fragile to begin with, having it manipulated so that my attachment to you was so strong I felt like I was going to melt down, was cruel. It takes some courage to even bring the subject up, and not only did I bring it up, I tried to explain how I felt and often asked for your help.

But once again under the guise of therapy, you sat there smugly and let me idolize you, care for you and think about you 24/7. I lost my concentration at work, home and mostly while driving alone. I almost lost my life as I nearly drove through the stop sign near your home. Sometimes my breath was literally taken away because of the intensity and strength of my feelings. "In my book", there wasn't a better, more flawless person. You knew I was dependent - you knew I was needy ... you knew I would do anything for you ...I certainly met the criteria for what you and Freud and all the other intellectuals say is necessary.

And just being treated like a person instead of a textbook case study, that would have ruined the therapeutic alliance apparently. Really? You became more the problem than the solution. I craved information to see what made you that remarkable person sitting across from me each session. No matter what I commented on, things I didn't know, you did. You knew everything. I plotted and I planned. Though I have to admit it was a challenge - like a mind game figuring out how to obtain the information I wanted. You know it wasn't done to be intrusive - maybe it was fueled by my OCD -I was, as always, looking for immediate gratification. I focused on finding out things I was curious about, and then when I did, they weren't important any longer, and I would move on to something else. I think that's the way a lot of my life is.

You took over my life, my thoughts and my common sense too. Hard to imagine a profession with more power over a human being. A group of professionals who place themselves above reproach - instill the perception of perfection - of infallibility. Never admitting to faults, mistakes, misjudgments, never dealing with sadness or regrets or shortfalls in their own lives - all the while dealing with those of us who have experienced all of those things and need assurances that we aren't alone. You think you are the only one who is crazy, who reacts a certain way, who can't manage emotions - who can't handle Life. That even therapists aren't perfect could make us feel all kinds of people have problems, even you and other counselors and therapists, but instead we get long pauses - silence - one syllable answers - and no disclosure. Why wouldn't we feel weak and inferior? Our therapist doesn't even think we are capable of being treated like adults and carrying on adult conversations and activities. We should be made to surrender, and weeping, look to this all powerful person (much like the Wizard of OZ) to make suggestions what we alone should do if we ever want to be normal - if we ever want to get well. Whatever that is.

It's all cold, calculated impersonalized educational theory and subjectivity. I feel like a fool. The things I've said, the emotions that have poured forth, they are real, but your reactions, probably every word you say and don't say, is scripted. GAD, ADD, OCD, Page 101 - Crazy Patient - 8-8:50 a.m. I guess I just feel disgusted with myself - manipulated and exploited - that I fell into the trap - the scheme. It was just a means to an end - follow the protocol, prove the theory but leave the patient in turmoil. Hearing this, you're probably thinking good - She's Moving On - Page 103 - 110. The End. HAVE A GOOD DAY.

****

I realize now I am going through the 5 Stages of Grieving. Apparently I am in Stage 2 - Anger. I am angry as Hell, because using your profession, the program, your understanding of me, the Freudian philosophy, and every other reasoning out there, you purposely caused me to feel the strong feelings and love I feel for you. You knew I was dependent on you for my feelings of worth. You promoted it, you encouraged it, you didn't help me when I asked for your help. You sat there smugly and just let it "all work out" - just like in the textbooks. Your lack of feelings outweighed my overwhelming, all encompassing ones. I nearly missed exits while driving. I sat at my desk and thought only of you. Have you ever had difficulty breathing because your chest is so heavy with yearning for someone? You literally took my breath away. I thought I was having a heart attack. I felt like I was going to suffocate. Thoughts of you intruded every hour of every day. My obsessions- my compulsions - caused me to spend hours on the Internet. It was a challenge. I wanted to know everything about this man I revered so highly. Must be an ego trip for you... so many feeling you are so important, knowledgeable, without faults or weaknesses.

You set me up and now you are leaving. You have every right to move on, but I'm left to hurt and grieve. Do you understand that, or is it just part of the Master Plan? Don't you understand that putting vulnerable fragile minds through this kind of unrequited love-like relationship is cruel and hurts those who need love and comfort the most? Don't you know your leaving is just like losing a family member? My God you know more about me than any other human being. I entrusted everything, especially the fragility of my mind, to you, and you wouldn't even share more than an occasional sentence about yourself. What would and could have become a great equalizer, became instead a great divider. Me, the child, the subordinate, the mentally ill patient. You, the God-like therapist, who after 50 minutes moves on to another mentally ill person, never having to feel what it's like to be in the throes of despair. It must be great to have the ability to form such tight boundaries that you can look at every person as just a case study, follow procedure and then at the end of each 50 minutes, care nothing about them. Next patient: J - Page 96 in Understanding your Deranged Patient ...

Yes, I care too much. I don't believe you care at all. This is obviously nothing but a business arrangement. I give - you take. Mentally ill people are a dime a dozen, right? We are your job security.

Would it have hurt our "alliance" if you had just expanded a bit on receiving the Christmas present from me - said you used something in the basket, drank the wine, won on a ticket - that the business cards were funny, or 300+ words were flattering. Really? You couldn't even do that for me? Was it really "encouraging me" or just making me feel that maybe I was a little creative, a little thoughtful, made good choices, found a nice theme, was considerate contributing to the Cancer Society(for reasons apparent to you I'm sure.) Or that you liked my Letters to the Editor. I didn't expect praise (or maybe I did), but isn't acknowledging the gestures, just something any decent human being would do for another? Maybe in just talking to you as a peer, I could have felt somewhat intelligent and could have shown you I'm not always a sniveling idiot - not always a failure - and more importantly, that I wasn't always crazy. I was just a person who could converse on some level with someone so much more intelligent and powerful than myself. I didn't want to rip your clothes off. Honest. I just wanted to feel normal. I haven't in such a long time. The most human emotion I ever saw - that slight irritation you showed when we talked about the person who said you knew when you bought the house you would be living next to a school. Would seeing you as more than one dimensional have worked against our therapeutic alliance? No, because you knew I would do anything for you. I had already shared all my emotions - you didn't have to protect privacy - I wasn't going to go "too far". Would sharing your feelings about the loss of your Dad or Step Dad or how lucky you felt still having your Mom alive have changed our relationship? It would have served as a common thread between us, since I had recently lost my parents and mourned them so intensely. Finding out about you whether in elementary school, high school, college, work, church, etc...what I found just made me smile and feel proud - maternal - like a Mom who had raised a great child who went on to achieve so many goals. It wasn't done to hurt or intrude; I was just in awe, realizing how fortunate I was to be with someone so special, so educated, so respected by others ... someone who smiled like a shy little boy, who could laugh and be so comfortable in his own skin, who I once looked over and thought I can only imagine you as a college student, hair parted in the middle, long, maybe an activist of some sort. Someone who married young and started a beautiful family, who was proud of his children, both of whom followed in their parents' footsteps becoming compassionate and successful. Why was feeling any of that wrong? I wanted to burst so often just because I had the privilege of being with such an amazing individual. Even now, believe it or not, as much as I will miss you, your happiness is more important to me than my own. The fact that you will be training others to follow in your footsteps and become kind and compassionate counselors assures me that someday you will leave a wonderful legacy that will continue to thrive through the decades. Because I know you deserve it, I want nothing besides your happiness. Isn't that what I deserve too?

Stage 3 - Bargaining

I want so little but I'm pretty sure you will say "No" as usual. I would like to see you a couple of times a year when we go to Maine, as long as I am detached enough to feel I can handle it.

I would love to hear you deliver a sermon. You are the minister. Please "tend to your flock" just this once. I'd also like you to record a short list of hints, for example "J, when you get upset, just breathe.". Or "remember such and such"...a mini therapy session whenever I need it. A discussion about a few of the questions I gave to you - person to person not doctor to patient - and a hug. Would that be too much????

Stage 4 - Depression

Been there - done that - will do it again. That's something I will have to experience and work through - whether it is with you, another counselor or with stronger medication.

Stage 5 - Acceptance

Yeah, right. Like there's any other option.

WINTER

So the months sped by. I was already becoming terrified of what the future would bring when I was "alone", yet neither of us really broached the hard subjects. We never talked about grief, but it was always "in the air"… it was palpable. But we never spoke of it. I couldn't embrace it, so I just denied it was going to happen, ignoring the obvious. During the winter, I began writing prolifically. I wrote about the subjects that were too raw - too uncomfortable - to discuss in person, but I could write about them and read them aloud to D. By doing so, he was aware of how I felt, but I didn't have to look at him directly and admit it. I just lowered my head and read so many of these essays and poems. I wish now I had raised my eyes and observed his reactions. Just one of the many regrets I've had since he left.

Like the leaves on the tree, I cling to a strong branch for support. Their colors will change - they'll soon fall to the ground. Darkness will settle in, October will soon be at an end.

Summer's sun has set - it's cold. But the chill is within - the warmth is gone…my world is shattered… my refuge is gone. With chattering teeth, I crawl under the covers and cry myself to sleep.

He's gone…and with him all my life's closely guarded secrets, emotions, longings and desires…but my respect, admiration and gratitude will never go away. I'll never forget. Never. My innermost feelings are hidden away in a special place that no one else can reach.

When times get unbearable (and they will), I'll retreat to that special place and ask : What would He do? He'd be calm I tell myself and forgiving. I need calm… and forgiveness.

I need Him I think. I can't breathe … I gasp for air …I'm drowning …waves of emotion rush over me. Please, I still need you…I'm mentally ill….please come back…I'm teetering on the edge…I'm losing my grip…who will catch me when I fall?

Then I wake up and remember he's gone. I vowed I mustn't " cry because it's over but smile because it happened ". So I fake a smile and pick myself up and go on. Probably. Or not. Either way, I'll survive. Unless I don't.

Maybe, someday I'll even live the life I think I want. Or I won't. No matter, time is running out. If the moment isn't seized, it will be lost forever and ever. Can I do it? Will I? Should I even attempt it? Why bother? I hear the voice ringing in my ears "You're a Quitter"…. a failure…you don't deserve to be happy … you've done nothing right…look at your history, Loser.

We'll see. Another familiar voice, just a little louder says "You know what to do - you've worked too hard for so many years - don't give up". Sometimes I've thought the only good thing about life was ending it, but now I realize the only good thing about life is living it. So today I whisper "I'll Try." I'll go it alone…I'll grieve …I'll hurt …I'll be sad… and slowly maybe I'll accept that my happiness has always been just up to me and no one else. I'll lower my expectation to zero and then there will be no way to go but Up. Maybe someday there will be more good days than bad. Maybe someday I'll get my special send off to Heaven. So many maybes - so many uncertainties. So much fear. I ponder can I do it All or am I setting myself up for the inevitable fall?

Maybe in a few months, when the trees turn green and Maine and the ocean beckon, I can stop by and check in with you. I'd really like that. But by then I will, of course, have moved on…you'll just be the "friend I used to know" - "Great to see you"…"Oh I can't stay"…"Places to go and people to see:…Oh maybe a hug just for old times sakes…50 minute friend we've got 30 minutes left - maybe we can make a Plan - another 3 months I'll be back again".

SUMMER

Time went on. The months flew by so quickly. The summer was in full swing. I was scared. So, as I have for most of my life, I decided one day I should just quit. I'd quit then and not get hurt by him leaving that final day. It took all the courage I could muster to stay. I thought it wouldn't be fair to either of us if I left without my therapy coming to it's rightful conclusion. But it was going to be so hard. Before I decided to continue in therapy, I read D this letter, a portion of which came from a most wonderful blog I found on the Internet.

Please note in sharing my writings, I have copied them over just as originally written. My writing is just like my thoughts - often jumbled and disorganized. Sentences often run on and become paragraphs. My thoughts and ruminations do the same thing. They continue on uninterrupted. I write as I think. This **may** not be the perfectly formatted book, but it's real. It's me. Often you will notice I mention the same "themes" in several places. It's apparent that subjects such as his lack of caring and his not sharing information with me really were "deal breakers" for me. And transference aside, I loved this man. Yes, he took the place of my parents and a spouse who told me years ago he didn't have a passion for anything (and apparently that included me). Like many men, he didn't like to talk about emotions, and as we began to lead separate lives, our discussions became non-existent. But with D, that was not the case. He was "within reach" (figuratively,) if I needed him. . He was fully invested in my care and well being. I mattered (at least for the 50 minutes he saw me). Sometimes I felt foolish knowing I had to pay for this compassion and caring, but at least it fulfilled what was truly missing in my life. Once I lost my parents' unconditional love with their passing, I was left alone emotionally. I cried often.

Dear D,

I'm sad. I truly am sad because I know it's over. I know I may never be ready, but as you said, you are "moving on", and I think you may already be there mentally. I'm angry at myself for allowing your reaction to the anniversary card to hurt me and trigger my 800 plus calorie breakfast binge. Expectations derail me every time. I thought I was doing a nice thing. I guess not, huh?

You've helped me immeasurably; certain things, however, I have to do for myself and I haven't. I've accepted I'm mentally ill. I will never like myself all the time, and I have to live with that. Hopefully I will have more good days than bad. Some days are better than others already. Today, writing this, is not one of them. You have done everything right... suggested all the appropriate options...listened to so much "Deja Poo". I can't even stand myself, because I truly do repeat this crap over and over. I'm sorry

I am needy, I need support, I need praise, I need someone to listen to me...always been about my "needs", hasn't it? How friggin pathetic. What I really need to know is why this damn fragile psyche of mine works against me.

I don't completely trust you. I have all the faith in the world in you , but I feel I am just a textbook case - a non-entity. It's just a game with you...I'm just the pawn. I get more understanding of the patient/therapist relationship when reading the <u>Making of a Therapist</u> or <u>The Heart of Psychotherapy</u> than I have gotten from you. You knew how I was happy and excited about that card. Apparently in your opinion, I couldn't make the card and concentrate on my own life as well? The little wedding announcement I had printed off 2 years ago when I discovered Genealogy.com. I told you about it then. I had Brett "burn" the 2 songs on the CD for you. It cost me nothing. It was thoughtful. It was given with a kind spirit. It was a simple Anniversary wish to you *both.   Too bad, just like in the past, you ruined my happiness by "shooting me down".   There are only 5 months left for God's sake. You couldn't just bend those boundaries a smidgeon? I'm sure you will continue to "let me down". Basically you will disappear off the face of the earth and never look back. I'm not even going to push the boundaries and stick around for a hug. You were just a figment of my imagination - a fantasy come true. There was that little crack in the façade when you shared about playing basketball with the Judge at the Y and your jury duty experience...but it was replaced this past week, with what came across as you being preoccupied ...there was something missing. Well at least we have something in common finally.   I truly think you are as sick of me as I am sick of myself. Really, who wouldn't be?*

Anyway, though I never planned it this way, I think I should cancel our appointment and call it quits.   You of all people certainly know I've always been a quitter. Before I get hurt or when I'm overwhelmed, I just quit. I love you with all my heart. I couldn't even say those words to my own Dad and Mom. It's hard for me to even say them to my grandkids - never to my kids except Beej and almost never to B. You have made all the difference in the world in my life over these past 7 years. Through the ups and downs, you have always been there for me. I think you are the BEST. Of course, I've told you that many times before, haven't I?

> *Whenever I'm lonely and blue, I see Dr. Seuss,*
> *Smile, and think of you.*
> *Is a baby bird this scared when pushed from it's nest?*
> *You can't imagine the fear I feel*
> *Detaching from the Best.*
> *You've given me safety*
> *When I was scared*
> *Shielding me often from daily cares.*
> *You were my safe haven*

When around me was in turmoil.
I always left your office with reason to smile.
Now that door will shut for good
And it will be rough
With no one else have I developed such trust.
You understood everything I'm feeling but can't say.
What will I do when you walk away?

Last but not least, I want to leave you with something funny I found while googling "how to say goodbye to a therapist you love". Not sure who the author was but it certainly speaks to my feelings. This patient's reaction to losing his therapist is something I can relate to, proving something painful can also be very funny. I hope it makes you laugh too.

"Recently, my therapist told me we had a limited number of sessions left because he is moving to another state and taking some time off from being a therapist. I was confused because, I guess I'd assumed that the therapist-patient relationship was an indefinite one, or at least one, that if it were to end, it would end on my own terms — perhaps with me rushing out of my therapist's office into the sunshine with my arms wide open ready to embrace life and love and happiness without crippling anxiety and depression, maybe while "Beautiful Day" by U2 played in the background.

Unfortunately, like most of my relationships, this one with my therapist is ending abruptly and without me feeling ready for it. (Abandonment issues! Hooray!) Obviously, I hadn't previously considered the possibility that my therapist was also a real person and might someday need to move on. When my therapist told me he was quitting being a therapist, I had many questions. Here are some of the immediate ones:

"Wait, what?"

"Wait, you're quitting being a therapist? But...but you're MY therapist! I thought this would go on forever and you'd be coaching me through my panic attacks as we grow old together! It was going to be romantic."

"Are you even ALLOWED to do that?!"

"What about all your patients?! I mean, I know I'm self-obsessed, but this time, it's not just me here."

"You're just going to abandon us all?"

"But you haven't heard all my f-cked up stories! And what about the fucked up stuff I haven't even done yet? There will be so many of those! Don't you want to stick around for that?"

"Is that it? You just drop off the face of the planet after everything you know about me and we live our separate lives never to speak again?"

"Can we keep in touch?"

"Is that weird?"

"Like, can we still talk? We used to talk so much and now there's no protocol for saying 'Goodbye.'"

"Would you want to be pen pals and maybe listen to my b-tching and moaning via letter?"

"Can we be friends now?"

"Are you going to write a book about me?"

"Seriously, why are you doing this?"

"Did you not hear me when I said 'Everyone always leaves me in the end'?"

"You can't just stop being a person's therapist! Haven't you seen The Sixth Sense? Won't one of your disgruntled patients just show up at your house and shoot you?"

"I'm not going to shoot you, no! I'm just saying."

"Am I supposed to find a new therapist now? I'm not going to liiiike anyone else!"

"What about all we had together?! All we shared? You're just going to throw that away?"

"How is it so easy for you to walk away? Was I the last straw?"

"Were my problems too intense? Or too ordinary?"

"Please don't leave me. I'm not ready."

DON'T YOU THINK A PERSON CAN CARE?

I had one last "bitching" essay to write before he left. Strangely enough this was one of the few times he commented on my writing (I think). I guess I should be happy about that, huh?

Early in the summer I had found a wonderful group of supportive friends at a local women's retreat on the Lake. We were like-minded women, all about the same age "finding ourselves". I cried every workshop that summer. Sessions with a Life Coach, during journaling, yoga and meditation, every class except Chinese brush painting, I cried. Every lesson, in one way or the other, addressed my impending loss. I was vulnerable. There was a deep seeded ongoing sadness that wouldn't go away. I wrote the following essay to express even more bottled up emotions, that were by now, simmering close to the surface.

It is easier to identify with women all of whom have their own problems - we are all equals - we've all been through the same type of lifetime barriers and now we are ready to overcome them - to find time for ourselves - to find peace within ourselves. Because in therapy with you I have had to be a subordinate, a less than equal participant - while you allow yourself to come across as perfect - that alone makes me a lesser person. And how much really can any man know about being a woman - about hormones - and trying to do it all - and what would you know about trying to make money stretch - living paycheck to paycheck - putting your kids first - helping them out - worrying about them - being ridiculed for your emotions.

Just like no man can feel the pain of childbirth, so too can you never identify with really any of MY life. If you have never had OCD or ADD or anxiety or panic attacks, then no matter what you have read, you can't know what the pain they cause feels like. I can't get across, even to you, just how intense these feelings are, and for some reason, that frustrates me. It's much like trying to express how deeply I feel about you. I can't find, or maybe don't know, the words...if I could just make you understand my feelings, then maybe you could understand Me and be able to reach me and make it all stop, and I could get better. Unfortunately, though you can empathize, you can't relate to these emotional disturbances, if you've never been there. See, being perfect, with a perfect family and a perfect wife and a meticulous home and having a second home and having prestigious jobs and coming from money and never being ridiculed for being ugly and fat, you can't identify at all with me. And even though you know my psychological problems, as well as my family dynamics or lack thereof, thus understanding why I feel the way I do about you, I'm guessing you truly can't imagine how much it hurts to be this pathetic and needy - how much it hurts to love you in the way I do and for the reasons I do. And then to know I'm going to lose you and be alone. I know I'm angry and I know I'm grieving already. This is the real me - I'm a bitch - ask B. I think the whole fucking thing started as an ego trip for Sigmund Freud and then just got passed down to every psychological practitioner as doctrine. Really he wasn't good looking and he needed women experiencing in his term "transference" to boost his ego, make him feel like a man and "serve as a vessel in which he could be powerful and in control.

Very gently he looked at me and said "Do you think that just because a person doesn't have the same problems, they can't care about another person?" He said it so softly, I knew he was referring to "us" and I whispered "Maybe they can." Later, after the appointment was over and I was alone, I cried. God, I was going to miss this man being a part of my life. I was sure there could not be - there would not be - another person so important to me in my lifetime

THE END IS NEAR

October 31, 2013. The day was here. I was nauseous. I sat in the car waiting for him to arrive and began writing down my thoughts and emotions, which I later read to D.. He was a runner; it was appropriate.

All those years she would always "run late" - this day, however, she finally was on time - early even. She wanted it over - she wanted it never to end. Over 7 years she knew there would always be an appointment card - a "next time". October 31st... that last next time was upon her.

The preparations were complete. Like labor she thinks there's no way to stop the pain except to feel it - to run with it - to own it. She wants to throw up - waves of nausea - difficulty taking a deep breath - but he had always said "Breathe" - her chest throbs - her eyes sting - it really hurts so bad - it envelopes her body and mind - she can't move. Yet she wants to run away.

This must be how it feels to run a half marathon. Mile 1 flies by...Mile 5 it's harder ...Mile 8 drained but continuing to push forward ...Mile 9 excruciating pain ...Miles 10...11...12...13 - no way to stop except quitting ...not an option...come too far...body and mind are exhausted...in this race there's no trophy at the end ... no onlookers to lend support - maybe for now just persevering - just getting to the finish line will be prize enough. The crowds are gone - the end is in sight - 50 more minutes - regrets - too bad there will never be another race - too bad the last runner is Me, she thinks. And no one at the Finish Line to continue cheering her on.

She opens the door - and steps out of the car - at last making her way towards the soon to be closed doors. The unknown awaits.

43

It was followed by the attached good-bye letter I had composed weeks earlier, but revised right up until I entered his office.. I wanted it perfect. It would be the last time I could tell him how I felt and how important he had been to my life. I hope he liked it. It took me 11 minutes exactly to read it to him. While reading it, I laughed. And I cried. And my heart broke.

Dear D,

I'm sorry but there may be a tinge of anger and/or hurt interspersed with the admiration and love. I know it's just part of the grieving process. You don't have to respond to any of it.

Over 7 years of our lives ... what an array of subjects we've discussed. What an array of feelings I've expressed; an even greater array of feelings I've felt. And you have changed not at all (maybe a bit more grey but that was to be expected after dealing with my roller coaster life over the years).

I may have told you once or twice before, I'm really going to miss you. Knowing you have been MY counselor - knowing I could come to MY "safe place" and always say what I felt and not have to fear criticism no matter how crazy I behaved; that there was always a calm presence in my life who would be there for me - just me - no matter what; having someone I would never lie to - whom I had complete confidence and trust in; who always provided a haven for me to be myself. It meant everything to me. It boggles my mind how much you know about me....more than any other human being does or ever did or ever will. And how little I know about you. Ok that part's BS ...it seemed to be the thing to write, but you know I can't lie to you!

I read in a magazine article that "our skin needs to be touched, our bodies need to be held, our spirits need to feel loved". Though I couldn't experience and enjoy those things at home, I could appreciate something akin to them mentally during each and every appointment.

You provided an atmosphere and environment conducive to change and projected a demeanor that inspired and motivated. You kept assuring me it was possible to change. You tried to help me focus less on my fears and anxieties and more on what could be accomplished, gosh darn it, if I changed my attitude and expectations.

You knew I always wanted to know if you cared for me, but you just ignored the subject and never responded whenever I told you about reading or talking to other therapists who said of course they cared about their clients. But the funny thing is, you never asked me what my definition of caring was...Does he observe the skewed thinking, anxieties and abnormal behaviors but sees through that façade, and realizes inside there is a really good person who once was intelligent, who's in a lot of pain now and is desperate to get better. Does he actually care if I get better (or some such shit...I write books, not psychology textbooks). I think most patients would agree that our most basic desire is just not to be a textbook case, but to be an individual. I wanted only to be a somebody, not just an anybody. I didn't expect to be special - I just didn't want to be "nobody special".

Since our last appointment, I found the "flaw" we always talked about. I wasn't looking for it - I didn't ever really want to find one - but when I received your e-mail, I realized I had lied. I really did expect you would see me a half hour earlier, because I thought after 7 plus years, for the last appointment, I was at least that important to you - that you could get up a half hour earlier and bend the rules just this once. But like everybody else, I really am and always have been, only a 50 minute customer- just a client - just a buyer - just a consumer of your services. No more, no less. What was it I read to you once: We expect more from others because we would do that much for them. Damn those expectations!

I can be empathetic, sympathetic and helpful to others because I truly care about them and want to help them in any way I can. Maybe that's another of my flaws, but if it is, so be it. You told me early on most people aren't worth worrying about. It shocked me when you said that, you know. I'm glad now that both my niece and BJ's old girlfriend, Cate, didn't go into the psychology field. They are sweet, caring, loving people. They would have been eaten up and spit out by a profession that sets people up to be completely vulnerable - and then to be hurt, all under the guise of helping them help themselves, while inflating a therapist's ego. You didn't like my "investigative work" but I didn't like to be unequal and inferior . Guess we are even now, huh?

I am at least fully aware of the irrational thoughts and behaviors caused by my OCD/ADD/GAD thinking - the ruminations and resentments - and that they are not the best options for me. Hopefully I will continue to work at getting them, and keeping them, under control. And if they (the OCD and ADD plus a side of anxiety) never become fully arrested, then maybe it would be enough for me to just try to laugh at myself, accept they are "ME" - that nobody is perfect (except you of course). In the entire scheme of things, they really won't matter a year from now or 5 years from now and if I die, they won't matter at all. If I can't change everything, maybe I can change some more of those things that have stood in my way for so long. Even baby steps are better than none at all. I think I've made pretty good progress so far.

The reason I wanted to do well and make it on my own was because I rationalized anything less would be disloyal - disrespectful - to you. You have spent so much time with me - been so good to me - in my heart and my mind, I didn't want to let you or myself down, even *though I've come to believe your philosophy is based on the 4 Tenets - Show Up, Tell the Truth, Do the Best You Can and Don't Be Concerned About the Outcome. You did everything right ...everything by the book ... now I just have to be able to follow through with what you've taught me. I hope I can. At least **I'm** concerned about the outcome.*

I have been so dependent because I needed someone to be there for just me, because nobody else was. Losing my parents was the hardest thing I ever went through until now, but I had you. I thought you were 100% in my corner - you gave me a "soft place to fall". I let myself believe you were empathetic - you got it - you "had my back". I always knew you were my security blanket - my safety net. Now I feel like a tightrope walker. If I fall, there's nobody to catch me. I needed to be seen; to be heard. I was and am vulnerable...vulnerability: baring your soul with no guarantees. I thought with you there was a guarantee of protection and safety no matter what. Brene Brown said it takes courage to be vulnerable. If that's so, I must truly be a hero. I was pathetic, and I'm sorry for that as well as crying every appointment and dragging this out so long... making you listen to so much Deja Poo.

I know I've been blessed, because I had a Mom and Dad who loved me and were the BEST (and screw a profession that wants to blame all our problems on our parents). I have 4 children who have become successful despite me being their Mother, and lots of beautiful grandchildren, who love me. I have good friends that like me for myself I guess. I've become involved in volunteering more, church activities and giving back - trying to be a good person and not make the same mistakes over again.

I guess I'm good enough. I'll probably never like myself, but maybe it's enough that others do. Maybe someday I'll start to see and believe what they see and acknowledge. At least I'm not a fake. I don't pretend to be anyone I'm not. What you see is what you get.

I feel so much gratitude - still feel I'm the luckiest person in the whole world to have had you as my therapist for over 7 years. I'm still filled with admiration and awe that I got to be with an Executive Director, Training Coordinator, Author, Adjunct Faculty, Ordained Minister, a Doctor of Education, an old LCSW, a Licensed Marriage and Family Therapist, a consultant for 12 Counseling Centers, not to mention a die-hard Red Sox fan (you really are a glutton for punishment, aren't you?). As I've said many times before,

WOW!!!!!

But you are so much more. So intelligent, youthful, active, sophisticated and worldly, thoughtful and compassionate, attentive and fully committed to your Family. You are a good and loyal friend - an athlete and outdoorsman with many passions - a scholar with many interests - a man with great passion for life. You are well thought of by the Clergy and the nonprofit community. I mustn't forget to mention that you are handsome and sexy; one could even say really "hot" for an Old Guy. A man who has worked hard his entire life and seemingly has it all - and I got to be with you for 50 minutes every 2 weeks. WOWZA! I don't know what I did to deserve you, but Thank God for emotional and mental illnesses!!!!!

I can't thank you enough for the opportunity to come to you. I will miss you, our time together AND researching you on the Internet. That alone may spark my next career move - becoming a private investigator! Or a process server - I could find most anyone - and their relatives - and their relatives' relatives - and their relative's homes - and previous homes and directions to...Ok, I don't want to expound on all my secrets and abilities... "I have no special talents...I'm just passionately curious."

Funny how I can feel that way about someone who says few words, shows no emotion, shares almost nothing, and lives in a "completely different world" than mine.

I would ask only that you read my "Book" - maybe on a long cross country flight when you need something to make you look busy so that fat lady beside you doesn't "talk your ear off" and tell you her problems (Oh, wait, that was me). The book is a combination of fantasy and reality, hopes and dreams, expectations and needs that could finally be met - if only in the pages of a book. And due to my inability to make decisions, the reader will have their choice of 3 different endings and an equal number of titles. I think it might be pretty good - or will be when I finish it and get some help with editing. Right now, I'm only half way there. I want it to be the one project I actually finish before I die. You will recognize a lot of it is based on truth (or what I wish were true). I hope you see the humor, appreciate the references and descriptions. Till the end, my "hero" remains "perfect". You know what? Maybe he really is. As much as I would like to know your thoughts about it, I learned long ago you would give me little praise or validation. After all this time, trust me - I really do have few expectations - it hurts less that way. All I hope is that you enjoy it and understand "where I was coming from" . If you read it, visualize the most beautiful client you've ever had. I'm only the storyteller - the narrator - kinda like Earl Hammer of The Waltons. Like you said about my Joy of Writing essays, when I stated I didn't need validation, "but you'd appreciate it". Of course, I would. But I will never know if you throw it in the trash when I leave your office; it won't matter really - it will be your loss - and my lost $25 to have it printed. I've lost more than that doing stupid things for you and other people I cared for in my life.

Saying thank you is not nearly adequate enough for what you and your counsel have meant to me. That's why I always wanted to give you the gifts. Because words weren't enough to express the deep gratitude I felt for the impact you had on my life. Unfortunately, the gift giving also became the times I hurt the most, cried the most, had my hopes dashed the most... the only times I considered quitting.

Still you'll have my thanks, admiration and love - I was the challenge you were above.

But I know this is not an outcome that can't be overcome. (Quoted from the Internet) " At first glance, it may appear to be too hard. Look again. Always look again." I'll be ok.

I know you'd tell me not to cry for you, but you know it's who I am...so please forgive me...I'm doing the best I can. Hard to believe it's over...I prayed to God there'd be more...it seems our story barely started...and now you'll walk out the door . I'm glad we had this time together, sharing stories for so long, seems like it just began, and before my mind can accept it, you'll be gone." (take off on some of my favorite Dr. Seuss quotes) Always remember (and never forget) when it's all said and done, it's been so real - it's been so much fun (He replied: "it has been, hasn't it?")

Everything that has a Beginning, has an End. Make Peace with That and All Will Be Well.....Buddha.

With all my love and thanks, J

P.S. I made myself tell you I loved you because it was so important to me that you understood my feelings ... to give those words a voice. BTW it really is love I feel. The dictionary says that love is "1. **Tenderness**, **fondness**, *predilection,* **warmth, passion, adoration.** *2. Love, affection,* **devotion** *all mean* **a deep and enduring emotional regard, usually for another person**...*love may apply to various kinds of regard:* ...**reverent adoration** *towards God or* **a person,** *etc.* **Affection is fondness for others that is enduring and tender, but calm. Devotion is an intense love and steadfast, enduring loyalty to** *a person...liking,* inclination, **regard, friendliness...***like...adore,* **adulate, worship.**" *Those words define love - define You - perfectly.*

THE END HAD COME

November was here now. He was no longer counseling clients, but he often was still in the area tying up loose ends. That was the tough thing. Knowing he was close by (only 2 streets away from my daughter's home, in fact), and I couldn't have any contact with him. I even went to two Open Houses at his home which was For Sale. It was so beautiful. I thought about him living there, eating in the breakfast nook, reading in the bright spacious den, sleeping in the bed in the Master Bedroom, and I was excited and envious.   But I also felt imprisoned by those strict boundaries, real and imagined, set years earlier. I knew in my gut I shouldn't have been there. I was intruding. I felt like a voyeur. I felt like throwing up, yet I walked through every room, sometimes twice. I **couldn't** stop myself. I **had** to do it. I **had** to be close to him. I **had** to feel connected, if only for a moment. I would drive up his street, see his car there, and panic if I spotted him outside. He mustn't see I still cared.   OMG, I missed him so.

On the date of my regular appointment several weeks later, I decided to write in a journal online and have a "virtual appointment" with him. It actually was kinda fun. It helped a bit.

8 A.M. November 22, 2013

This will take the place of an appointment with D. It has been 3 weeks - it's driving me crazy not seeing him .

I realized I really don't have anything I need to share with you, except how much I miss you. I only cried on October 31st and one or 2 other times. You know, I should have recorded more of our appointments. I am having such a good time listening to them - of course hearing your voice - but just remembering things I'd forgotten. My one regret is not taping them all - maybe I should *have asked, but what if you shot me down - I'd have had nothing at all to remember you by. Now I have a "TEACHING" picture on my screensaver, your calm and soothing voice and advice to listen to every day and The Book to write down my feelings and thoughts, as well as to visualize our appointments within the pages. I won't always "need" these things, but right now, I do. Ok? Feeling the way I do - restless and in limbo - antsy - at loose ends - has spawned creativity in my writings and that is good. I have ideas... I always have ideas.*

Still almost impossible to believe I might never see you again. I'm pretty sure I'll end up lurking somewhere - some time - hard to believe a person can be cut off completely like this. Just seeing you once in awhile would not be like seeing you every other week - it wouldn't be so harsh a termination - still can't believe you really care, or you wouldn't have done this. Why not just say if you come to Maine, just stop in. Why shut the door forever?

Don't you want to know D, if I'm okay? Well... at least read my book updates - cause if you do, you'll know how I am doing. Ok? Please.

Lord, I hate your profession sometimes - it's so rigid - why couldn't we just be friends and send a note back and forth or just let me stop by. I wouldn't DO anything wrong - maybe it would even show how far I've come. What if I saw you again and I actually found you didn't look so "perfect", so handsome, so sexy (okay, that's probably not likely) - you just looked like another human being. Wouldn't that be a good thing? How will I ever know? I should have asked why was your hair different that last appointment - I like the middle part - more youthful. Just saying...

FYI, I wrote sad poetry in Church today with tears in my eyes. It was a challenge since I was ushering!

I don't have anybody to talk to about this loss. I feel like a fake sometimes - not really caring - not really listening to other people - just going through the motions of life - of being a wife - a mother - a grandmother - a friend - and deep down I really don't give a shit about much of anything anymore. Except going in, turning on the computer and looking at the screensaver of you. I know, I'm pathetic. Sorry.

You know what things I think we really could have done differently? Of course, taping appointments is the biggie - and sharing more about yourself would have thwarted my unrelenting quest for knowledge (sound like some sort of a scholar, don't I, instead of a stalker) and I sure should have thought to sit in "that chair" - I think it might have made a difference. I shouldn't have wasted time on idle chatter when I really had so many questions. I wish we had delved more deeply into why I am such emotional bombshell. Face it, those are the issues that caused me the most angst. My emotions were always working against me, weren't they? Frustration caused much of the self esteem problems, didn't it? We never discussed what being happy meant. I read somewhere it meant being content - that's one of my problems - I'm never content - never satisfied - with myself or others. And I live in the past, don't I? But the past wasn't always good. I was nervous and anxious back then, but I had my folks, so those memories always overshadowed the other ones that weren't so great, of a shy, ugly young girl & young woman..

And then I found I might be a highly sensitive person and that would make sense. I thought ok - were I not sensitive, then I might not be writing - something I have a passion for. Note: I am having trouble describing the "Hero's" body in The Book - I'm running out of superlative adjectives. Any come to mind? This is kinda fun - just writing whatever. What was it I would tell you: "I'm going to jump all over the place" and you would smile and say "I noticed" - you were funny lots of the time. I wish I had taken a little peek to see if you have chest hair - for literary research purposes - I'm not a pervert you know -I just want descriptions in The Book accurate - just like giving the heroine curls and a thin body - it's my book - I can change things up a bit - so the "hero" will have chest hair cause B did - probably still does - I just don't have "access" to it anymore....

I really found out lots about you, didn't I? Only once (or twice really but only once I will share) did I feel a little guilty - like I overstepped a boundary. Did I tell you that at the first Open House I felt really weird like I shouldn't be there but the second time I didn't feel the same remorse, cause I wasn't a patient anymore. I have a tote bag I got free from Oprah Magazine which is the same print and color as your bed shams. Coincidence? I think not. It's the perfect home - meticulous and immaculate. I loved the addition room - so bright and cheery - like my "new" room that we got, thanks to you.

Shoot I really am crazy.....
Gosh I liked you.....

Pertaining to The Book...funny thought: I hope he respects me in the morning after he reads it. To be honest, I thought I would leave in certain references to locations, names, etc. so you might write and tell me I couldn't publish those personal facts; then I'd know at least you read it. Of course, I would never have published anything to invade your privacy or hurt you.. I think to myself...I do have a vivid imagination, don't I. I paid attention - have a pretty good memory for some things -some of my own personal memories from a loooong time ago - haven't even got to use my $.25 garage sale find yet. The sexual content of The Book is pretty well complete and I'm working on dialog (I don't think I spelled that right, did I? Maybe I did -the red line for an error didn't appear) - gotta have communication in a relationship - it can't all be about the physical aspects, right? You gotta be able to talk to each other. Don't I wish! Don't you think life *experiences should count towards a Counseling Degree???? If so, I could have a Ph.D by now!*

Anyhow, I think my 50 minutes is nearly up. I'll make myself an appointment card - 2 weeks ok with you? - and I'll finish up with a funny quote or story…..and then very simply leave (this page) as I always left your office, saying a sincere Thank You. Should I send you the $8.00 co-pay? (Wonder if I should have gone off all my Meds so soon????)☺

A few weeks later, I decided to try another "appointment". I still was not really in a "bad place". I was still in denial. The finality of the loss hadn't set in yet. I enjoyed thinking of past appointments and writing the way I talked - disorganized and scatter brained. I opened my mouth and words just rushed out. I had so much to say and there was always just 50 minutes. It was never enough.

SO…I've been thinking (are you scared yet?). I'm not really in a bad place - at least most of the time - I just wanted to talk with E about some unfinished business we never discussed. And of course about You.

I'm an okay person I guess. I know in my heart it's true. I understand unmet expectations. I think of things I could do, but don't do them, when they are just reactions, not actions. I volunteer lots. I understand irrational thoughts are irrational. I'm not taking any "psyche" meds. I'm funny. I'm a good enough writer. I'm willing to sacrifice to continue in retirement. I don't go shopping. I'm outgoing and can talk to anybody. I'm a good friend - try to be empathic and available. I work tirelessly. I love being around people. I'm independent. I don't always do what everybody else does.

I learned to say I Love You - maybe inappropriate under some circumstances but really was it???? I think not. I was in awe of you

- had warm feelings of enthusiasm - etc. Trust, faith, respect...of course I loved you.

I would have few of these transference feelings if B had only been affectionate and given me some emotional support. I wasn't looking to be "somebody special" - I knew you had lots of other clients - but I didn't want to be just an appointment card..

Look at the things I've done right: Making lists; journaling an appointment when I needed to talk. I haven't contacted you. I've asked for help from E - others wouldn't. I like her a lot. It's such a good feeling being "back home" again. 50 minutes goes by so quickly, and I have so much hurt and grief to still work through. It's reassuring I can tell her anything...even more than I could tell you sometimes... because it would have been embarrassing, or uncomfortable, or because we just didn't talk about such topics. I could make it on my own and will, but not as well as after this is settled once and for all.

I admit for the first time even you might not have been perfect.

There were things you could have shared - things you could have done differently. Rev used a phrase in church "I find your restraint offensive..." Hmmm. Such a void in my life. You could have been more open - more humanizing - Aaron Beck said it is ok for therapists to share - but you were with me all the way- you were there - you didn't terminate me till the very last day possible - you let me vent whenever I needed to - you let me be me.

You could have stopped harping about why I keep looking up info on you and your family. You knew it upset me when you sounded annoyed. I wonder if you taped our appointments or just had an awesome memory. You could have let me tape the last one or at least asked me why I wanted to, and then you might have understood - it was a simple request - not sure why you weren't comfortable with it.

And why the Hell didn't I speak up and insist - actually express my indignation. I never did. I respected you and your opinions so much...I knew they usually were good for me, so I listened and tried to follow your suggestions.

Do you therapists care? All the books I read say you do, but I never saw a hint of caring about the "outcome" - if you had just laughed about some of the gifts or said you used them, what would have been the downside? You had some analytic reason you told me the last day, but you were wrong - I give gifts to people I like - not just family - cause I enjoy doing it - seeing their happiness - because they deserve a special gift. You reading more into some of my actions hurt me the most - made me want to quit. I nearly did several times. By being so boundary driven, I never knew if you were concerned about me getting better - or even thought of any of us beyond the 50 minutes - if you think of us now - if you ever check to see how we are doing with our new counselors. I didn't want to contact you to ask which therapist you would recommend I see, cause I didn't want to admit I wasn't strong enough to cope on my own. That you still mattered to me. That I still cared. I didn't want to be pathetic anymore. Was it at all hard for you to say good-bye to so many people. I'm glad you moved though - I couldn't have handled termination if you were still living and working here. The closest you came to saying you cared was when you said you wouldn't treat a client if you didn't like them. How forthcoming was that, right? I needed insight - I wanted to know why I was like I am - what could have caused it - of course we talked about it, but I don't think we delved into it enough- a lot I wondered about we didn't pursue and it was dropped. That was my fault. I just jumped to other subjects. I like being intelligent enough to find out things about you - things that were a challenge, but showed I was pretty darn creative in my research. I liked those few times I was an adult and not a child-like adult.

You knew I agonized about transference, but yet all those years we never really discussed it or the reasons I felt that way, did we? Seemed strange as though you weren't comfortable with the subject. Or maybe you sensed I wasn't, even though it engulfed me for years.

I got a perfunctory hug at the end - never felt a shirt that was a softer cotton or cotton blend - LL Bean,? Eddie Bauer? Timberland? Probably Macy's. Most proud: I didn't quit. I hung in there - it took courage to stay - it wouldn't have if I had just "walked away". E told me you tell your trainees to just let clients go if they say they want to leave because they know best. Really? If I had quit, you wouldn't have asked why or asked if I was sure I was making the right choice? You wouldn't have cared if I walked away? Why does that not surprise me.

I "went the distance". I wasn't crying as you saw me walk out the door for the last time. I smiled and said Thank You just as if there would be another appointment - just as if my heart wasn't about to break.

You could have worn an ugly shirt - or admitted one bad habit - or have gotten old - but you just got better and better. I loved You, idealized You, idolized You. Thank goodness for my writing. Remember how I joked that you were welcome to come as "eye candy" on my book tour. Would love to know what you think about my books...my poems...my writing. I guess it's better to get no response - no approval- than to get disparaging remarks. Criticism from you would have devastated me. I worked really hard, you know, but I won't "take the bridge" if I don't hear from you (remember who taught me to have low expectations, right?). I'll continue writing and hopefully publishing, but it would have been nice to just have a little input from somebody whose opinion mattered so much to me - past, present and future. Notice the books tend to be about you? Wanna be a policeman or a cowboy or a lawyer in another book? I could write a trilogy.

Imagine seeing YOU - the Executive Director with so many initials after your name. I saw the "Upper Crust", didn't I? I have so much gratitude for that. I couldn't have asked for anything more... I couldn't have asked for anyone better. Miss You Lots!

Hard as it is to believe, this was a better "termination" (isn't that a harsh word? Sounds like I was fired from a job) than if he had stayed in the area and just announced our therapy was ending. I could not imagine voluntarily choosing to end our alliance, to lose that feeling, to give up the safety and protection I felt when I was with him. I understand the reason for my need to see him. This terrible grief may be difficult for a "normal" (whatever that is) person to understand. I'm an individual who yearns for - who craves- attention and lovingness in her life - someone to understand my deep seeded emotions - someone to help me sort out the threads of my past in order to understand my present and future - someone I don't need to control - someone I can see as perfect - someone who didn't need to change for me. D wore all those hats and more.

I knew I was needy. So many of us are. I couldn't handle even perceived criticism. He rarely criticized. He was my anchor in the storms. I was in awe. I'd have done absolutely anything for him.

I wanted so much to be "better". I told him I understood Michael Jackson wanting to sleep so badly he would risk his life. Drug addicts who wanted "that good feeling... that feeling of being normal." I understood them. And hoarders. Not being able to make decisions about emptying their homes of unneeded clutter, disposing of possessions. I understood them, too. Actually, I am them...just to a much lesser degree. It's frustrating as Hell.

EXPERIENCING GRIEF

By December, I had decided to see a woman therapist at D's counseling center. For obvious reasons, when D & I discussed the possibility I might see another therapist, we both agreed it should be a woman. I couldn't take a chance on suffering such intense feelings ever again. I was grieving so deeply. When he had asked me several months before he left, if I would be interested in seeing another counselor, I said "No, because I've already been with the Best". Needless to say, I had changed my mind by late November. I had to talk to someone. And E had trained under him, so I knew she would be a kind and empathetic person, which she is. My, it was hard walking in that building the first time and seeing "our" office with someone else's name on the door. I nearly vomited when I saw his title changed from Executive Director to Staff Therapist several months earlier on the Center's website. Oh no, that couldn't be. He was so much more than that.

I had continued writing though, and I read many of these essays to E. What I couldn't comprehend was how intense the anger was. It came in waves. He had abandoned me, broken our "alliance", left me alone. Why wouldn't I be angry at him? There is nothing rational about anger...or love for that matter. Many of these feelings came out as poems. I hope that my readers can feel the depth of emotion, imagine the anger and despair, as I read them aloud (with special inflections) to E. My voice cracked, and I sobbed inconsolably for what was and might never be again.

Before it got better, it got much, much worse...
His personality - his character - his entire being was like expensive dark wood - bold and beautiful - polished - solid - dependable - upright - never a crack in it's façade.
She missed him so - it was as though her heart -her soul - had been

ripped out. Waves of nausea rose in her throat - she tried to cry out but her chest felt as though it would explode - she couldn't speak - only lonely sobs escaped - wet, salty tears trickled slowly down her burning cheeks.

She wanted to scream - Remember you're supposed to HELP ME! Help Just ME.

I HATE YOU… I LOVE YOU… STAY AWAY… COME BACK …

You know how you hurt me - why didn't you just LEAVE - GET THE HELL OUT OF HERE - Vanish - Depart - Withdraw - Move On - Move Out - Hit the Road - Shove Off - Beat It - Scram…

HERE *is* **MY** *Life -* **You** *don't have any right to it anymore.* **You** *hurt me.* **You** *abandoned me.* **You** *left me. ALONE.*

You nearly destroyed me, you know. That pain - it won't stop till I know you're not going to be parked in **that** *driveway - or in* **that** *parking lot - in* **MY** *City - in* **MY** *State - in* **MY** *Life - in* **MY** *Heart - GO - PLEASE GO - NOW.*

Or I'll have to keep loving you -and keep hurting - and never be able to GO ON - - ALONE.

PLEASE Move On - or I Can't - or I Won't - Be Able to Heal and Get Over You.

If You Must Leave, Just GO - (but always remember, I've Loved You So).

And then there were the letters I wrote but never sent (thankfully).

Dear D,

"Didn't you hear me? Wasn't I loud and clear? Weren't you listening? You who makes your living listening. Didn't you hear the pain? Why were you standing there at the end of that driveway? When will it ever end?

You know what? You weren't that person I used to know. This must be how a New Hampshirian (is that even a real word? If so, did I spell it correctly?) looks. Too much outdoorsy camper - hiker…too much green.

Now I have to hold my breath - for how long - for how many days- till I can breathe again. Damn you. Now I feel like throwing up again - I've drawn blood from my fingernails - AGAIN. The longer you drag this out, the longer I feel sick and tired and abandoned and so very, very sad.

Don't you know you control me - my emotions - my very being - being this close but yet so very far away.

One more appointment with E (insurance runs out) and I have no one - all by myself to cry and hurt so badly - to grieve and to try and figure out how to go on - Alone.

My God, my paper is stained - wet with tears over YOU. What have I done to myself? Caring so much about you - caring THIS much about you. And neither of us actually caring even a little bit about ME.

Every time I know you are near, it's like the pain comes again in waves, and I'm vulnerable and pathetic and an orphan - again.

I always told you the truth. Remember I told you that? I was wrong. I told you I would be okay. I lied.

I can live without you. There are books, tapes, self-help books - what I really need is just your validation - your approval - your caring - just a little longer. Please. Remember when I said I didn't need validation from my writing group and you said "but you'd appreciate it". What? You expected I needed validation from 8 people I just met and didn't care about and not from someone I trusted and admired for more than 7 years. Was that realistic???

You couldn't just bring me back to an equal level, could you - even to the end - Patient - Practitioner - Paragon - Pedagogue - Pathetic - Pain - Pitiful - Puke - Perish.

Parting - or more accurately termination - didn't have to be this harsh and painful. You could have given me permission to say Hi - send a note - a joke - you could have said I'd like to know how you are doing - an e-mail - funny obituaries from the paper - even a smiley face. THIS is preferable to being kind and caring and compassionate? You could have said "you could stop in and have an appointment when you are in the area"...I probably wouldn't have, but at least I would have known you might actually have cared about me. Just for a little longer...please.

Even a doctor who does amputations follows up with his patients. Was this any different? You don't think this was the same? You cut off my lifeline - you broke my heart - one day you're there for me - but then 50 minutes later you don't give a shit?

Are you so perfect you are heartless...don't be concerned about the GD outcome, right?

Can you even comprehend how angry I am at you? How is it possible I feel this way about somebody I love so very much. Remember I wrote that chapter about a fine line between love and hate? I think I've crossed it. Damn you!!!!! Seven plus years I sat there never arguing - never questioning anything you did or said - now I want to scream and shake you till you understand how badly I feel - till you feel MY pain. Why didn't you help me prepare for this?????

I know what I will do. I'll turn to the only real friend I've ever had. FOOD. I've already gained 15 lbs. since you left. I'll eat and for a few minutes the hurt will go away until it is replaced by the usual self loathing. Who cares, right? Toughen up, Bitch.

*I'll listen to the appointments I taped. I'll listen to THAT man - the one who joked with me and made me laugh and always feel better when I left his office. You know what? On those tapes you sounded nice. And concerned. I laughed so often. I cried a lot too, of course, but at the end I laughed - A LOT. And that made me consider, maybe he actually did like me. He sounded like he didn't mind me being there. In his own way. He stuck with me; he was present, and listened, really listened, and joked and was serious when necessary. Maybe those things were his way of showing he cared. Maybe he's not so good with sharing it - boundaries you know - but maybe I should be happy that this man can make me smile just listening to old tapes. You can't be sad when you're smiling, right? Thank you for being there for me - just me -**until you weren't**.*

Only then I didn't realize that man was only real for 50 minutes. A quote from The Velveteen Rabbit *really resonated with me: "Real isn't how you are made," said the Skin Horse. "It's a thing that happens to you. When someone loves you for a long, long time, not just to play with, but Really loves you, then you become Real". Apparently, that only happens in children's books.*

Sometimes I feel sad I grieve a man who only listened to me because I paid him. I mean it was only a one-sided relationship, right? It wasn't real, was it? You grieve people who die. You didn't die. You weren't family. I like to think you were a friend of sorts. A friend is someone who knows all about you but likes you anyway. If I believe that definition, maybe you were my friend - my 50 minute friend at least.

The words just poured forth onto the paper. I typed furiously trying somehow to make the paper absorb the deep feelings I was trying to convey. It will be up to you, Dear Reader, to decide if I succeeded.

Dear D,

I sit here surrounded by people on all sides - in church - listening to Rev - but thinking of you. I am still sad remembering you. When will there be a respite from these feelings? A few hours of drug-induced sleep maybe, but then another morning dawns. But even before the sun rises, I wake thinking immediately of you. Desiring you...trying to remember you...or rather, the feeling I had with you. I want to replicate it, remember it, experience it again but I can't. I squeeze my eyes tightly shut and concentrate so very hard, but it won't come back. What I yearn for is gone. Only in listening to the tapes can I laugh and cry and feel happy - connected again.

I ponder this morning...what is normal? I don't know. I know I'm not, but what makes other people - those people - normal?

I have to imagine they are... content, satisfied, happy, not overwhelmed. They don't obsess, let their thoughts control and sometimes overtake their lives.

They must have focus and intelligence and hobbies they enjoy and projects they actually complete.

They don't hone in and ruminate. They don't panic. They use coping skills (common sense) to solve problems and live their lives.

They don't always think of the past, their mistakes, their regrets, worst case scenarios.

Yes, this must be "normal". Normal's not me.

Dear D,

I think I will be better by summer. You will be gone for good by then, and I can get back outdoors, walking and gardening. And I will go to the Lake retreat again - maybe I'll even see another eagle!

I think maybe The Book was too racy, huh? Sorry. I'm thinking of writing a blog if I could learn how. There are others like me out there. Misery loves company, right? Would like to publish The Book. My target audience would be patients - those suffering (and it truly is suffering) from transference - those who fantasize about their therapists. I know there are lots of us.

It's time to be happy, isn't it? Why do I keep repeating that phrase but in reality, I don't embrace it - own it - accept it. This grieving is so all encompassing. It's so emotionally draining. So many things are so overwhelming because I'm emotionally disturbed (I guess that was supposed to make me feel better about myself- better than mentally ill, huh?). Life goes on, right? It's not like I've been happy lots and now I'm depressed.

I feel better when I am busy - concentrating on anything except you and my loss. Maybe it is getting better little by little. Maybe when I see E, stepping into THAT building, makes it too real - makes it worse rather than better - or maybe it makes it real - and I need to experience REAL - REAL LOSS. I should feel grateful for the time we had together, shouldn't I? Grateful, not grief stricken. But not yet. I guess you couldn't have joked with me the way you did if you didn't like me a little. Unless you were really good at faking it. For 7 years? I choose to believe you did like me- and you did listen - and maybe you cared (a tiny bit) and maybe you knew how hard this would be for me, no matter how I tried to be upbeat at the end. Maybe deep down you knew the truth.

For so long, I yearned for peace and serenity. Normalcy. Calm. I wanted to be soothed and comforted and told everything will be all right. That I will be all right. I'm so tired and frustrated by my "condition". Even before I was diagnosed, I knew I was different. You know, my self esteem is nearly non-existent. How can any of us - the mentally ill - feel good about ourselves when we know we are ill

67

- mentally not physically - but it must be kept a secret, shared with only a few. There is no Handicapped Parking - no sympathy - no caring - no support for us . We are alone and hurting.

But once every 2 weeks you entered my life; I felt good about myself. The clouds lifted. The sun even shone. I smiled and shared and gained confidence in myself. If you valued me and my thoughts, then maybe, just maybe, I wasn't worthless and pathetic. You didn't give up on me, so I didn't give up on myself. You always told me I could do things on my own. I was capable. I could be responsible for my own well being and happiness.

You never let me down. After you left, I felt it was important that I not let you down. I could see the changes in my thinking -because of you. I believe I'm thinking clearer. I'm beginning to "know" me pretty well now. I handle upsetting situations better...because of you. I write lists of things about myself I embrace and those things I'd like to change. I think I'm finally ready. I'll do it this time, D. I promise. For you. And for me. I want you to know you made a difference in my life. I want you to be proud of me. That's all I ever wanted. I want you to, I suppose, care about "the outcome."

You had so many opportunities to say "I care - I'm concerned about you." I am so mindless - I didn't look up - can't remember your reaction to the scrapbook - or my good-bye letter -I didn't even know what your couch looked like I sat on all those years - so why should I expect to remember exactly how you looked - or sounded - or made me feel.

Dear D,
I thought things were getting better, but today is tough. Not because it's the weekend and I drove by your house, but because it's the weekend and I didn't drive by your house. I shouldn't go to Jen's - it's too close - I can't stand the knowing - and the not knowing

apparently - of your presence. My chest hurts. I feel so nauseous and sad. And of course I listen to country music, and I am even sadder, because each song - each lyric - speaks to me. I find I don't give a shit about anything or anybody sometimes. I want to be alone - alone on a beach in Maine. But now you've spoiled that pleasure of mine. You've moved too close to my peaceful place - it's replaced by just wanting to see - to contact - you. I'd be willing to sit for hours just to see you walk by in the distance - just a glimpse of the man I "used to know" You wouldn't even have to see me.   I'm pathetic. I don't care...\or maybe I do. Today, you know why I didn't drive by? I remembered your advice once about confronting my brother "what would be gained by it?". And I couldn't think of a positive thing, except if you weren't there in that driveway, I could take a deep cleansing breath and go on for another week. But if you were in your driveway, as happened the preceding week on a Thursday, when I didn't expect you'd be in town - I would dissolve in tears, begin to eat mindlessly, chew my fingernails to the quick once again and accomplish nothing.   It would be 9 days till I saw E to bring me back to center. I wasn't sure I could do it by myself. Damn you, D. Just once more I wish I could hear a simple Good Morning, J and walk down that quiet hallway following you into my happy place.   Country lyrics play inside my head "He was a most uncommon man".

Dear D,
What do they say? Fool me once, shame on you - fool me twice, shame on me. I did it again, but this time I'm not angry at you - I'm infuriated with myself...my reactions.

What an asshole. Why did I drive by? I held back almost 3 weeks - I never even visited Jen on the weekends - had B do the grocery shopping for me - put off errands till Monday. Then on Thursday I drove by - and was shocked the blue car was in the driveway. And I began that downward spiral of ruminating, devouring nearly a month's worth of fingernails I had calmly grown. GONE. Yep, bleeding again. What is frigging wrong with me. Things were getting better...it was a good day. But Jen had to have me come over to babysit - and it was all downhill. Damn. I cannot imagine why I think of you from the second I wake up till I go to sleep. Thank goodness I don't dream or you'd be in them too. I try so hard to remember the hug, the way you looked in the office, walking down the hallway. Why can't I?

I need 2 things: to have you leave for good and know for certain the house is sold - you won't be coming back. Maybe even see another family in the yard unpacking their things. And I want so badly for you to let me know you would like to hear from me. That would show me you might still be interested in my accomplishments, my goals and my desire to succeed. But I wouldn't want your validation if you said it just to "get me off your back". If you didn't really feel that way, then I wouldn't want to know. I wouldn't want to hear from you. Previously if I didn't hear from you, I would have taken it personally. But you know what? If you don't contact me, it's your loss. I guess you must not think I'm any good - my work is any good - isn't worth commenting on- certainly not worth pursuing or publishing. In the past, I would have given up and quit writing. That's not the case now. You know, I made you - oh, I'm sorry - the "hero" - so wonderful, so perfect, so many references only you would understand - terminology- words that came straight from your mouth. In more ways than you can possibly know, it's a love story... a tribute...and an Ending. I won't stop writing though. If it's not good, I'll just revise and make it better - if only for the opportunity to prove to you and myself I can actually finish something I start. Would have been nice to have a little positive feedback... an unselfish gesture for someone "you used to know", who needs to know she wasn't just a Friday time slot. But don't worry...I have low expectations.

I was beginning to understand my thought processes when I wrote this:

I remember when my Mom died. Every week my mind would automatically count down from the time of her death - it's been one week since Mom died, two weeks since Mom died, then a month, 3 months, six months, then by the year. January 7, 2007 - I knew that date by heart. The saddest day of my life. But as the time spans became longer, the pain began to lessen. Tears would still come 4, 5, 6 years afterwards whenever I spoke her name, but the good memories began to overtake the terrible loss. Never forgetting her, but death didn't invade my every waking hour, every day, every week. My mind was less consumed with the actual anniversary date but I always knew - felt in my heart - Mom and Dad were with me.

I noticed the same feelings when you left. I remember panicking at 2 weeks - this should have been my appointment - I felt the pain of losing my "rock" replayed. I felt anxious - sad - really bitchy - occasionally bitter - and compounding the sorrow, I turned to no one - I had thought I would, but I didn't - not even my Woman's Group for support. Instead, as much as possible , I turned away from them - from my friends; they couldn't or wouldn't understand. I was certain they were thinking Get Over It Why Don't You - so I didn't "bother" even them - I cut myself off - I would go it alone - I was strong - I'd get through it - life goes on, right? It goes on but not smoothly - not without rocky moments - not without waves of sadness - not without reeling from virtual punches in the stomach - in the heart - in the very soul of my being.

I'd even thought about contacting you and casually inquiring "If I hypothetically decided to see a grief counselor, who would you recommend?" We'd talked about it before so it wouldn't have been exactly coming out of "left field", right? But I didn't. Even with you, I thought if he didn't care to give you an extra half hour of his valuable time, why come across as pathetic and needy now? Why let on. Why let him know you still care? Why admit to him that his leaving left a hole in your heart? Why admit to him he mattered.

Losing a therapist is a very individualized grief. It can't be compared to death or being left by a long -time friend or lover. It's very isolating - not to be shared. And as you will remember, I shared everything "in the day". But this was different.

You know that scrapbook I made you when you left? The scrapbook I spent innumerable hours and money preparing, as well as the research involved in finding the information to compile it. You know, the one I was so proud of. I rarely ever looked at it after I finished it, except when I brought it to show you. And when I did, it was with a feeling of accomplishment. Otherwise I packed it away in a drawer and forgot it was even there. But I had gained the confidence to make others for my "real family". Well, after an appointment with E and showing her half the scrapbook, I came home, carefully took it from my bag, and threw it away. And I cried. I made it for YOU. And then I threw it away. I felt empty inside afterwards. I couldn't look at the overflowing wastebasket.

I contemplated why I created it. True it was a tribute, but deep down I wanted you to know what a good job I'd done. I wanted you to see how much info I'd found. I wanted you to say " You certainly did a good job - look at the myriad of things I didn't even know you could find on the Internet" (1234 47th Street was a stroke of good luck if I do say so myself). Always wanted your approval I guess. I'd put away your pictures weeks before in the top of my closet. It was, I guess, all part of the closure…a lot of reflection, introspection, loss…the unfairness of grief. It was a project like so many others to keep my mind busy. I wanted you to see how much time and especially how much thought I'd put into it, just because it was the history of a very great and respected man - a "man I would miss so *much". Believe me, 5 minutes of me turning pages while showing it to you our last day, didn't do it justice. It was special from a very thankful, grateful person who would no longer be a part of your life. If only you had taken it when I initially asked you to look at it in your free time. Too bad...once again, your loss ...it was really good!!!*

I'll keep a new scrapbook. But this one will be a record of my "talks" with you. They'll be the real me. Just like our appointments, except you're not there...only my memories . You won't be with me to joke, or listen, or guide me. I'm on my own. E and I will have to get through this together. It won't be the same. I don't know if I can do it, but I'll try. What have I got to lose, right?

You know I was always afraid of losing people I loved...sometimes I wondered if there was anyone out there afraid of losing me. Guess not, huh?

Gaining courage (but not necessarily good judgment), I decided to send him some of my writings. Of course he never replied. I never gave up though. I wanted so much to feel he missed our time together, that he actually was concerned about how I was doing.

Here's one I didn't send. The anger had reared it's ugly head again.

Dear D,
I am still having a tough time with your leaving. I write you letters (ones I don't send), make up fake appointments and type them up. I did something really hard yesterday. I went through the remainder of the scrapbook and threw it away. I cried. I worked so hard on it - I don't even know why. Or maybe I do, but the reason just makes me all the more pitiful.

I brought your picture back out to my desk a few weeks ago. I glance at it and the appointment card for September 27th once in awhile.

I went on a hike and saw an Eagle...had such a good time. Afterwards I thought of you, and wished I could have told you all I've done and my plans for the future. I'm keeping really busy - for the right and wrong reasons. I like myself better mostly. Except when I think of you and realize I can't move on. Just cause it was easy for you, doesn't mean it is for me. Of course, I loved you. Obviously, the feeling wasn't mutual, as it couldn't be...I understand that. I understand transference. I can't help but question why you didn't even really care about me - or probably any of your clients. Just 50 minute customers. Hard to acknowledge - harder to accept.

You know what? I wrote that long letter apologizing for intruding on your private life. Didn't send it either, did I? Know why? Cause really I don't feel guilty or care if I'm intrusive. And guess what? I probably won't stop. Only thing I'm sorry for is that I told you information I found out, and that I wrote several of the disclosures in The Book. Mostly mentioning family illnesses and a direct quote from your step dad's obituary. And I probably won't tone the sex down. Why should I? It's not like you care...ever cared - one way or the other. Or that you will ever give me credit for writing two books or even admit to reading them. Bet you didn't even think I'd finish them cause I'm a Loser? You had nothing to worry about, right?

I really enjoyed reading Jeffrey Kottler's book <u>On Being a Therapist</u>. I think he cares about his clients - and I like he's got his own issues. Same with Rob Dobrenski, and his book <u>Crazy - Notes On and Off the Couch</u>. How come so many therapists write and say you can share with clients and make yourself more approachable and you wouldn't? You didn't give me much credit, did you? Even at the end. You always made sure I was "in my place". I was the patient. I've read a book where the author admits therapists like the power and being emulated and being in control and admired. They thrive on it. I figured as much. Why else would you let me think you were flawless - not shatter the mystique - not make yourself real.

I enjoyed therapy and your company. I read in some book or magazine, an article that said even though in the past, a therapist was supposed to be a blank slate, in actuality patients observed things so it was no longer possible to be that "neutral entity". Of course now with the Internet, we have access to so much information about other people, which was never the case in years gone by. I picked up on every nuance and then jumped to my own conclusions. I knew when your allergies were bothering you, and I felt badly for you. I would see you look out the window for more than a quick glance - or stretch and move in your chair - and I would immediately think you must be bored or not paying attention - and of course that it must be my fault. I saw the bruise on your finger one day. I wondered what happened but I never asked. I would watch you run your long fingers through the part in your hair and figure since I was always the first appointment of the day, you were fresh from the shower and it had just dried. I loved to watch you do that. Your shirts were always crisp - your pants perfectly pressed - trained to be appealing, weren't you - though I know you hated that terminology.

I loved your sense of humor and your jokes and your calmness and that I never left not feeling better, except on those days you confronted me about why I researched you or admonished me for giving you a gift, and then I left wanting to quit. I was strong to stick it out though, wasn't I? Maybe. I didn't cry when I walked out the door that last time. Though I wanted to turn around and say "I really did love you, you know", I hesitated for a split second, then said something stupid - Good Luck - and walked out the door. I should have turned around and hugged you one last time. What was the worst that could happen? Not like you could have told me I couldn't come anymore, or I stretched your GD boundaries. You couldn't even give me that extra half hour in the morning. After over 7 years. If I had mattered, you would have. That's when I knew I didn't.

I cared about you so much and your happiness. I even commented that final day it must be hard for you saying goodbye to so many people, and you shrugged and mumbled something. Maybe it wasn't. Maybe you had termination down to a science by then.

You couldn't possibly relate to me anyway. You were rich, came from money, highly educated, put your kids in the best colleges, had beautiful homes, nice cars, name brand clothing, married to the same woman seemingly happily for 43 years...you couldn't really know how most of us "disturbed" clients feel. You can hear the pain, but after all you're trained to block out the suffering, right? Except for your Dad passing away when you were young, you've led a pretty privileged life, haven't you? I admit you worked long and hard and have achieved many great things though, for which you deserve much credit.

Days and months flew by. I kept writing. I'll condense some of the letters, picking out a few key paragraphs in several of them. The pain just didn't go away. I kept thinking of him each and every day so many times. Obviously, some things that bothered me intensely were repeated many times in the different writings.

Dear D,
Isn't it time to be happy again? Finally this phrase is the key one I adopted to help me lessen this grieving after you left. My emotions were so raw for so long. Instead of getting better as the weeks went by, it got worse. It was 24/7. I couldn't escape the pain. I tried to fill nearly every waking hour of every day with mindless activities to try to wipe you from my mind.

To the outside world I'm sure it seemed to be working, but just below the surface I was constantly in turmoil - riled up. My OCD stirs me up. Remember you said those words to me. I wanted to see you so much. I couldn't come to grips with why you wouldn't allow me to continue having appointments in New Hampshire. How could you know this would happen and not help prepare me for feeling abandoned and alone. I knew it would be hard, but it turned out to be unbearable. Even worse, I couldn't comprehend how it was ever going to get better. How do you heal a broken heart or worse yet, a broken spirit?

Then at 15 weeks out, I knew what I had to do. You were gone, the house was sold, the new people had moved in and the property already looked different. I was upset they weren't taking care of it like you did. And that's when I told myself, "Idiot, Just Don't Go There. No, really, JUST DON'T GO THERE. You don't need to go down that street - to put yourself through this nightmare - anymore. There's nothing to be gained from it - anymore."

I said "Self, you know that project you've been working on for months? The one he probably doesn't think you'll complete. Well, I'll show him, I thought. I will complete it - in fact, I'll do even better. I'll complete it - and get it published - and market it out there for everyone to see, and he'll see I'm not pathetic and needy anymore. I'll be a success - not a loser like he expects me to be. I'm better than that. And you know what? I'm going to prove him wrong. I'll change some names, tone down some of the sex, but I won't QUIT! You'll see - I'M NOT A LOSER ANYMORE! JUST WATCH ME!

I bet there aren't a lot of counselors who have books written about them. Flattering books. Books filled with love and respect and gratitude. The only thing missing - nobody here to say "Good Job".

When I write it feels normal - I feel normal - like an appointment - like you're still here. I talk - you listen - things get better. Yes, it's like an appointment - except it's not.

77

Dear D,

I'm sorry I've cried so much and complained so much and loved you so very much.. Other than my parents, I've never had anybody to take care of me and listen to me. I hate being so friggin unstable. I hate I let myself get so involved and never thought how it would end - that I would hurt so much. I'm conflicted. I'm torn. I'm so confused. I don't know what to do. I don't want to leave E, yet I know it's probably time. I cry thinking of leaving. I don't want to be alone with my mental illnesses... my emotional disturbances . I don't want to give up my safety net...I want to know somebody listens to me...understands me...knows I'm a good person, who is challenged every day by my emotions ...chemical imbalances...someone who understands how difficult it is trying to be "normal". If I leave I won't have anybody who knows I try so hard but still screw up so often. It's like an emotional hug coming here. I can't get over you and it frustrates me so much. I think of you non-stop and the pain overwhelms me. You know how I feel? **Like a cocoon burst open but no butterfly appeared - there was just an empty space inside - the butterfly had died preparing to spread it's wings.** *I have talked to E about these feelings, hoping they might lessen. But they haven't ...instead, they've multiplied. I miss the relationship the "fantasy man". The Book makes you real ... makes you care...makes you mine. You exemplify what is missing in my life. If It (and we both know what It is), wasn't missing, "You" wouldn't need to be here now. But that's not, and will never be, the case.*

THOUGHTS FOR A YOUNG THERAPIST

Lucky E. Now she gets to hear all my pathetic essays to D. But the following ones were written specifically for her. She is younger, very pretty, less experienced than D, actually empathetic and caring I think, or as much as anyone in her profession can be. I guess I yearn to make a difference in someone's life. I wanted so much to give her something to remember about me...about clients...about what a deep impression a therapist makes and how they influence clients' lives. We had been discussing my strong attachment to D, and she asked if it was like a crush. This was my reply:

*I agreed with you this longing is like a crush, but after reconsidering that term, I realize it is too simplistic. This is such a strong attraction, such a strong alliance, that it has now become an obsession. It is all consuming. I'm compelled to binge eat, chew my fingernails to the quick and research D. I **must** accomplish my goal of seeing him just once, or I won't be able to stop. It's been that way with everything. Getting a picture, taping the sessions, seeing the inside of his house, finding out how his Dad died...I **had** to. I couldn't stop. Please believe me, I wanted to. This is not just me speaking but also shows up on blogs I read. This kind of emotion is so strong we would be willing to break our marriage vows - we will grovel - become inferior like you want us to be - we will beg and plead and cajole - we will live with constant frustration - we will sacrifice our self respect and our self worth. We'll do all that for just one snippet of attention from you. How pathetic is that, right? If you haven't been there, you can't imagine. It effects every moment of my life now. It makes me sad - worthless - reinforces I'm a Loser.*

Sometimes I feel embarrassed I grieve a man who only listened to me because I paid for him to do so. I mean it was only a one-sided relationship. It wasn't real, was it? He didn't die. He wasn't family, but I like to think he was a friend of sorts. A friend is someone who knows all about you but likes you anyway. I guess that might be true. He said he didn't take clients he didn't like. How could he have known that first appointment that he would like me. What would he have done, I wonder, if he didn't. How would he have "terminated" me then?

I appreciate you told me he did care about me. Remember how that made me smile. It cheered me temporarily, even if I didn't believe you. Sorry.

If you take nothing else away from our time together, just remember how deeply and profoundly a therapist can impact a client; how not allowing follow up can be devastating. The pain you can create, as well as the joy you can inspire, by giving praise when it is deserved. A writer I read online said "Therapy doesn't heal...Love does". Be human - be authentic - be genuine - "hear", really hear us. Be imperfect. Be caring and mean it. Share - some personal self disclosure would make us more equals - would make us see you as a human being - not as in D's and many other counselors' cases, an awesome God up on a high pedestal that will never topple in our eyes. A status we can never attain - that we don't deserve for ourselves. Once again, as George Weinberg commented: "The higher the pedestal, the further you'll fall." Consider the plusses of a patient who is unfocused and in the throes of deep emotion taping appointments. They have been my greatest resource and happiness.

****

*E, You haven't been a therapist long enough to have had thousands of clients yet, so I would like you to always remember one thing. I could be the poster child for the impact a therapist has on a patient. And of the pain losing someone so special can create. Someday under a similar circumstance, remember and don't hold back showing you care because as I read recently, "Therapy doesn't cure a person, a lovingness does". Nobody ever would choose to be this emotional, and needy and pathetic. **Nobody would ever choose it**. To have a mind that challenges you and to never feel normal is tough. Some people have physical challenges and disabilities - we have mental ones. And they never leave our minds clear. It's like they are just beneath the surface and without warning burst through and throw our world into turmoil. If you have cancer or heart disease, or any of a myriad of other disabling diseases, people feel sympathy for you. Not so mental illness. There is always - spoken or*

80

unspoken - a stigma surrounding it and often those who don't have, or won't admit they have, any mental health issues just act superior around those of us who do.

*D left and I never heard "I Liked **You**" or "It was a pleasure working with **You** over the years and I **will miss You**." The statements he did utter were generic. He could have said them to any client. Probably he did. Maybe I did want to be special. That he would say he was proud of me was too much to ask for, but what about "I'll miss you - I've enjoyed our time together" or "I liked you as a client **and** a person" or maybe "J, I think you're a good person - you'll be okay, but I know you will miss me and I'm sorry for that". That would have made me feel so special. Sharing "I appreciate the fact you think I'm perfect, but really I'm not. I drive my wife crazy sometimes too." would have made him human. Do you know what a difference those words would have made for closure. I would have been so happy knowing he really did like me, care about my feelings and my future without him. That he truly did understand. Seven plus years and I get a "It's apparent to me today, you've done a good job for yourself". Really. Thanks (I guess). When I gave him The Book after telling him the week before I would never know if he had read it... all I wanted to hear was "Of course, I'll read it...and let you know how I liked it". As always, I got no response. No commitments. No promises. No healing.*

Why would telling me why he became a therapist (it was on my unanswered list of questions) have ruined our "alliance"? Or if a past patient had changed his feelings about certain things or impacted him. They seemed like logical questions - something a friend or acquaintance might ask in conversation. Why couldn't I be treated as an adult at the end? Why did I always have to be denied any type of gratification? Can you truthfully tell me that hearing how great you are and being on a pedestal isn't an ego trip for a therapist? Come on. He never denied it or even showed a flaw, so of course, I was in awe of him and his life. He knew how I would experience loss. He knew how I had experienced my folks' passing and next to them, his leaving would be the hardest thing I'd have to experience and work through. Leaving me like this...is this the way therapy is supposed to work? Is this a good termination?

81

Do you think it's ok to send him some cartoons once in awhile? Do you think he will look at them? And maybe smile. Or does he just block out everything and everyone he has counseled? Other therapists leave the door open - let their clients stay in contact - treat us like human beings with feelings. Is it truly just a job? Geez, even at my old job, I worried about my customers personally, as well as if their orders were delivered, etc. He did tell me early on that most people aren't worth worrying about. Is that true? Shocked me cause I never expected that from a minister. Do you think he meant me, too? A lot of the books now say a patient truly can love their therapist because of the way the client observes their demeanor, their actions, their genuineness, their empathy. It doesn't have to be just because of transference, right? I mean people who aren't patients have told me what a "great man" he is. That when he walks into a room, people don't even have to see him to feel his presence. Why wouldn't I care for him deeply after spending so much time with him in the sanctity of that small office for so many sessions?

****

We had an interesting conversation, E and I, after meeting together nearly 10 months. She asked if I trusted her. I replied:

Been thinking about your question whether I trust you. We have a different relationship, thus I have different feelings about you. Under the circumstances, that's a good thing. I definitely feel comfortable enough with you to be vulnerable. Being with you is like being with the women of my support group at the Lake. I'm more able to see you as a human being. You are more intelligent and more learned than I am, but still I feel more equal...less inferior... than I ever did with D. Obviously, feeling I'm on an equal level is very important to me. I've called you on the phone. I never called him. Though I never asked directly, I knew that would not be acceptable. I didn't fear your disapproval either when I burst into your office the day I received the first "proof" of this book. I never would have done that if it was D. I was excited and elated and YOU were the only person I wanted to share it with. It was only for a minute, but that's all I needed. You seemed to truly care I had accomplished this goal. I wanted to hug you so badly, as I would a friend. It felt so good to be so happy, but I didn't. You know why? Because I know what boundaries are and I'm cognizant of overstepping them. I knew it wasn't allowed. All "the books" say so. Boundaries were the only aspect of my relationship with D where I felt fearful - intimidated - like I was walking on eggshells. I was so afraid I'd do something "unforgivable", he would chastise me and then tell me to leave. With D, I was afraid to infringe on his tight boundaries, so I rarely even "tested the waters" for fear he would not allow me to keep seeing him. I think that's why I never argued with him about anything. I thought at any moment he could terminate me. I couldn't chance that happening.

With you, I feel supported. I think you probably like me okay. Most people do. Of course, I'm not crying and blubbering when I interact with most of them. But in the back of my mind, I don't trust D, or you, or anybody else in your profession. I've read way too many books, as you know...I know too much now about how to "treat a client" and much of it seems to be one-sided, unfair, manipulative and cruel. It's very hard now to imagine a therapist who is actually authentic and genuine. I don't think you can get the textbook shit out of your mind...it's always, For this, Do that and NEVER be concerned about the patient or the outcome. I have low expectations now of true honesty between us because it's not part of your training. YOU can't be honest and genuine because then YOU might become vulnerable and only those of us who are mentally ill can be put in that demeaning position. You are protected...you aren't allowed to share with us the Real You. I'm sure D repeated that point many times while you were under his supervision, didn't he?

You make many of the same empathetic comments each week and they are totally appreciated, because I need that (perceived) understanding of my loss. I need to be told I'm not abnormal...that's I'm not "crazy"...that I'm not pathetic... that my thinking isn't irrational. I'm just experiencing real pain and real loss, because there was no real "closure". I know you will be there "during my journey toward healing", no matter how long it takes. You're here to help me, at this particular time, work through the painful finality of a forced termination. One I never wanted. One I can't accept. One I didn't deserve after all those years. You've come across as warm and caring.. I couldn't ask for anything more. You have a unique perspective on my loss, as you knew D and trained under him. Others wouldn't have that kind of connection. I need connection desperately. I look forward to being with you each appointment. Sometimes I wish they were even more frequent.

I can't imagine how many things go on in a counselor's mind while distancing yourself, stepping away, analyzing and observing mentally ill patients with our warped thinking and our inability to change, get better and get on with our lives. And then, of course, it's necessary to put into action the "Therapeutic Plan". You know, what the "books" say you should do - must do - must say- in order to change "our" distorted mindset. **I've been thinking that therapy is similar to an autopsy. If you dissect a body, split him apart, cut deeply Into his heart and other organs, remove all of his outer skin - his protective covering - he then becomes just a skeleton of the person he once was. He is no longer the same person that was loved at one time by someone. He's become a nonentity - a nobody special...no longer an individual but just a tag number. He no longer has a "soul". You have destroyed his very being in the name of science, while stripping the "specimen" of his dignity, so the doctor can examine him under the premise of determining what was wrong with him - what caused his "death". In the medical professional's mind the "outcome" justifies the means. But does it really?**

Because I'm very comfortable here and appreciative that I can come to you, I guess it matters less if it's textbook - "cookbook therapy". No matter what kind of response it is, you're here for me and that's the most important thing. That's all I need for now.

You're a woman, you're much younger, you have your own issues, I'm sure, and that's fine with me. What makes me happy (and relieved) is I don't see you in a parental transference position; you're just a nice, friendly presence. I don't imagine you as perfect or flawless or far up on a pedestal looking down at me. And guess what? That's the way I like it...that's the way it should be in a "therapeutic alliance". I don't have the need for you to necessarily be proud of me - to show your approval - though when appropriate, of course, I appreciate it.

With D, as I've come to understand and accept, he took the place of my parents after their passing. I loved and adored him as I did my parents. I was very close to my Mom, in particular. I believe now, I suffered from some separation anxieties - abandonment issues - from a very young age. Why else would I throw up every school day during kindergarten after my Mom left me off, until finally the doctor told her to take me out of school that year ...to keep me with her at home. I was afraid - fearful - at school. I was safe and protected when enveloped in her love. My folks didn't even leave us to go away alone on a vacation until I was 16. When I went away to college, I was very homesick for such a long time. When I was married and we came home to visit, I cried each time as we left.

The years sped by. For 27 years we lived next door to Mom and Dad. They were a constant presence in my life. When they died only 8 months apart, my world was shattered. By then, D had come into my life. He was there to help me through the sorrow and loss. Now HE had become the "constant presence" in my life. I was important to someone again. I had nobody to be there for me except him. So, yes, he did become the parents I no longer had. I discovered I wanted him to be proud of me like my folks were. I still do. I was ugly - fat - wore glasses - was shy and awkward. But not in my parents' eyes. Just in my own. The perception still exists. You know what's weird? For some reason it was important to me that he didn't think I was "crazy". Dumb, huh?

I'm sure you can imagine a little kid jumping up and down calling out "Daddy, Mommy look at me. Look what I did. Aren't you proud of me? You're happy cause I was good, aren't you?" When the parents say, "Yes, Tommy, you did very good...we're very proud of you" the child feels elated...feels special. I had the same desire - need - for that approval from D. I begged - groveled - for his attention - approval - validation. I just wanted to hear I "did good" and for him to mean it. I thought if he was proud of me, then there must be something good about me, so I could be proud of myself. Had that scenario ever occurred, my self esteem would have soared. I'd have felt cared for once again. Look at the volunteer activities I participate in. My favorites are the ones where I get thanks and accolades for my work and myself. That's why my job of 34 years was so toxic for me - no approval, just criticism - thus no self esteem - I couldn't do anything right - couldn't do anything well.

I totally was in awe of D. I needed for him to replace the love I no longer could experience from my parents, as well as the feeling of intimacy I no longer received from B. When I look at D's picture, I still feel that sense of being held tight - protected...that feeling of safety. Especially when I look at his chest. I can almost feel the strength - the power -the comfort he provided. The "emotional hug" I'm now missing.

Long ago, I wrote an essay about having researched transference and I read it to D. As I left the session, I stopped, looked up at him and practically whispered "Did I say anything wrong?" and he shook his head and softly replied "No." A weight lifted from my shoulders. That was a tough appointment admitting how I felt about him - how important he was to me. It's still not easy.

E, Do YOU think I'm crazy?????

HALF A YEAR HAS PASSED

Hi,

I need to apologize to you. I've had time to think of many things, to reflect, to self-analyze and believe it or not, I see more clearly now.

I apologize sincerely for all the research (which some might consider stalking and lurking). I did, indeed, cross the boundaries. And I compounded the indiscretions by including much of what I learned in The Book.

In my own defense, I do have emotional disturbances (a direct quote from an astute therapist I once knew). But that's still not an excuse for my intrusions in your life. It was such a strong compulsion - obsession - addiction. I just couldn't stop. It gave me a "high" when I thought I had done well - when I accomplished my goal - no matter how long it took. You (and your life) were apparently my drug of choice. I'm sorry.

Reflecting on my actions, I'm trying to figure out exactly why #1 I had this fixation and #2 why I must have wanted you to know all I knew - all I had accomplished. I surmise it was because like a little child, I wanted your approval - your reaction - your attention - good or bad, huh? I wanted you to be proud of me, because I had set a goal and figured out a way to accomplish it. Guess not, huh. Sorry.

*At the time I didn't feel I was doing anything wrong. Of course it's easy to justify actions in the moment. I just wanted a connection I guess, even if it wasn't real. I'm not apologizing for loving you *(the Internet says anything over 4 months is love, not infatuation - and you know I believe everything I read on the Internet!), but rather for not respecting your personal boundaries. I just couldn't talk to you about those things; I just couldn't. Now I regret I didn't. I'm sorry.*

If I was too scared or intimidated to tell you in person, then I just put it in The Book or the scrapbook. How pathetic. E says I use "pathetic" too often - that I'm not - but I think she's just being nice. She told me she trained under you. I told her then she trained under the Best.

I didn't think I could walk in that building again without you there, but it's still feels like "home" - just the other end of the hallway. I am still trying to work through and understand that you can't allow yourself to care about your clients. For awhile I fixated on why you weren't comfortable with me taping the last appointment. I guess I caught you off guard. I could have protested, admitting I'd taped others, but I didn't want you to be angry with me that day - not then - not ever. It would have helped me immeasurably, but you didn't know that. I've learned to accept what is without needing to understand the reasoning and logic behind it. I think I might be growing up. I would have been so happy to just hear "I'll miss you too - but my door is always open - I'd really like to hear how you are doing" but that wasn't to be. I guess you are "trained to be appealing" but it's not part of the textbook training to have or show any feelings or emotions. It's okay. I understand. I read a lot of psychotherapy books you know. Probably too many. I "know the drill".

You know Beth Israel is starting a new pilot program to open up mental health providers' notes to their patients. That would have killed me. I would have known I was a textbook - a nobody special - and it would have been there in black and white. Would have been worse than my appointment with Kim, asking me when I knew I was mentally ill.

But on the bright side, because of the tape where you told me to get rid of cookbooks - 100 a month - I did indeed pack up 500 cookbooks this past week and donated them to the library. And some self help books too. I'll get another dumpster soon. Either that or have a garage sale and say Everything Free. Finally it is time to do what you encouraged me many times on the tapes (and in sessions) to do. At last I'm ready. Instead of being mindless, inattentive and unfocused, I listened to those appointments and it finally sunk in. Better late than never I guess. So many things I didn't process in the appointments - didn't "hear" - didn't assimilate - I understand now. I was too busy talking to take time to listen. Even in absentia, you're making a difference in my life. Thank you. Bet you didn't consider the possibility that might happen, huh. I was surprised too!

I wanted you to know just how far I've come - I didn't let you down - I remember what you told me. Just like the lady at the beach picking up the starfish, you "made a difference to this one."

I've read over The Book many times since you left. Once again, I apologize. Not that I didn't warn you, but maybe it is too graphic, too personal, too invasive. I realize I wrote it specifically for you. And me. No one else would "get" the references, the terminology, the jokes except you. I'll revise. I won't quit though, ok?

BTW, in real life and during our appointments, I didn't have those "impure" thoughts. They were just based on long ago personal memories. Honest. Also BTW - you know the heroine has curls and is light enough to be picked up and carried…it's my fantasy book…don't they call that poetic (or creative) license or some such verbiage. Mostly I would look over and think God, he's so intelligent…so amazing…so awesome …and maybe occasionally, OMG he's so sexy. And always, I'm so grateful to be here.

All these things aside, I bet most therapists don't have an entire book written about them. A book filled with praise and gratitude. A romance novel. A tribute. A love story. The invitation still stands for the book tour. I've worked so long and hard on my books. I love what I'm doing, but there's still so far to go. But as long as I don't drop dead (or get hit by a car collecting bottles) anytime soon, there's time.

In retrospect, I understand much of what I wrote exemplifies my yearning - my craving - for affection. I made sure at least the "heroine" got to experience what I will never have in my life. I live vicariously through her I guess. The Book is like my baby...I don't want to let it out of my sight. I've read it time and again, when I want to feel loved and protected. Though I thought I wrote it because it showed the control I wanted of dying (in real life also of course), I didn't realize till several readings how often I wrote variations on "he promised he'd never leave". Maybe it was my way of working through the termination, huh? You brought that up once, and I immediately dismissed the idea. Now I understand that was probably the case. Damn. As usual, you were right.

I was amazed how angry I could feel in the past months. How could I be so angry at someone I cared about so much. I couldn't wrap my mind around it. I couldn't believe the intensity of my feelings of loss and abandonment. I wish I had asked for your help to prepare me for it. Or maybe there isn't any way to prepare to experience grief. You just have to work through it. They say time (and writing) are great healers. We'll see.

To add insult to injury, you were advertising your services in trade magazines and on the website in search of new clients. Really? There were so many here who wanted you to stay, but you left us to "grovel" for new patients. Or so it seemed to my warped mind.

I read a quote in that advertisement that said "Dr. S said he works until the immediate situation is successfully diffused, and focuses on assisting the patient learn how the issue developed in the first place, whether it is a behavior or a void in their lifestyle. The ad continued: Dr. S says "When I am with a patient, my goal is to restore their lost or damaged sense of a full presence in their life. Helping individuals to embrace life and release concerns about those things out of their control is the most gratifying result of being a therapist." What BS! You weren't too worried about me having a "full presence" in MY Life or about the "void" I'm experiencing. You left ME to scrounge for new, exciting clients. Damn you. (This may be the irrational thinking you once explained to me.)

I hope you don't mind I sent this. In the 12 step program, isn't one of the steps apologizing to those you've hurt? (No, I haven't taken up drinking, though it's a thought!).

Still know I was the luckiest person - patient - client - ever to have been allowed to keep coming to therapy with you. Wonder if those NH clients have realized how fortunate they are yet.

*Thank you for being with me all the way…from beginning to end…**you never left me, until you couldn't stay**. For that I am eternally grateful. You made me feel empowered when I felt helpless. Again, thank you.*

I'll enclose a couple more chapters and some jokes. (Saying Goodbye to your Therapist says that's okay to do). Hope you don't mind. Of course you can throw them away, but really aren't you just a little bit curious? You should be. Take care.

I couldn't imagine he wasn't missing me and our appointments after all this time. How could a person not want to hear about my mental health issues and family dysfunction? I certainly missed our "relationship". Maybe, I reasoned, now that 7 months had elapsed he would have "softened" those boundaries. So, I sent him a letter (a synopsis of which follows).

Dear D,

We are going to Maine this coming week Sunday through Wednesday. Would it be possible to meet with you when you are in P on Tuesday anytime for an appointment or even in M Wednesday on our way home? Will enclose all the reasons some therapists say it's okay. I understand you may not agree. Maybe you could trust me - give me the opportunity - to be an adult who could handle it and not fall apart - to finally feel like an equal human being. You know, to "put me in a new chair". I truly believe if I could see you in a different environment - your new "home" - not as the man I idolized for so long, but just as a caring human being - I could accept that if you're okay, I'll be okay too. I know I have to finally leave the protection and safety I've felt in therapy. I probably am "the guest who overstayed her welcome" and must also move on. I've come a long way, and I'd like to share it one last time with you, because you are the only one who knows where I started from and the mess I was. And I have a couple of questions I never was brave enough to explore (nothing about you, promise).

I've learned a lot in this post therapy period. In writing this, I didn't want to come across as begging for "scraps from your table" (saw that on a blog recently and loved the analogy). I'm better than that, but it would have been nice to feel a "good closure"… a "good termination", with it being on my terms this time. That last 50 minutes rushed by, and I was mindless about so many details of that last session.

I hope you like my poems. You - and experiencing grief - were great inspirations for my writing. Please read them. I think you will sense a happier person…all because of YOU!

You know my e-mail address. I would pay full price for the appointment of course. If you don't respond, then I know not to bother you again. I hope I haven't overstepped my boundaries."

It only took a few days to receive the following reply by e-mail (I guess he really did know my e-mail address). Needless to say, I was devastated. This was not the hoped for outcome. I immediately called E, sobbing and needing to hear a friendly voice who would understand how badly I felt. He truly had abandoned me. Ignoring the request would have been better than responding, rejecting the idea and "closing the door forever". He didn't care. Probably never did. Or so I thought.

J,

I received your packet at work today. Thank you for your kind thoughts and the update on your progress. I am very impressed by all that you have done and are doing for your own benefit and health. I am sure it has been challenging, though I can sense from your comments that you are feeling proud of the changes you are making. That also pleases me to know that you are feeling better.
*I fully understand your request for a session when you are in the NH-ME area next week. Unfortunately, I will be on the road for my other counseling responsibilities Tuesday-Thursday so it wouldn't be doable anyway. But, even if I were in town, I do think that our situation was different in therapy than the documents you quoted in your sent materials. Our therapy work ended because of my life decision to relocate, not because either you or I decided your therapy should be concluded. That is why I strongly encouraged you to continue to work with E as your new therapist (he never said that, but that's neither here nor there). Based on what you wrote to me, I can sense that the work has progressed well for you. **I could not have wished for a better outcome.***

So, though the pages you sent underscoring how therapist/patient relationships "should" transition once therapy ends are quite clear, I believe that they do not really address the uniqueness of our situation when I moved. That is also why I wanted you to know many months ahead of my leaving so that we could discuss it at your pace.

94

I hope that you have a great trip and time with your family. I wish you well, J. **Thank you for the privilege of working with you.**

Well, THAT certainly was not what I wanted to hear. It didn't make sense. That was only his friggin opinion. None of the words mattered, only the fact he didn't want to see me ever again. I was devastated. So I wrote the following poems (note: "the privilege of working with you" fit nicely into the rhyme). Also note the intense anger. I was seething.

Bastard. Fuck you. You are wrong. Seeing you would have made me strong.
You f-----g Bastard...I loved you so.
How could you do this?
Didn't you know?
You knew I would miss you
I'd be all alone.
I put on a brave face so no one will know
Just how much I miss you so.
The days are long
The nights longer still
I miss you today
I always, always will.
How could you just walk away?
You knew how badly I wanted you to stay.
I can't go on. I hate my mind.
You discarded me just like an old dime.
Didn't you care what you did to me?
Leaving that day and abandoning me.
Now I realize it never was about you and me.
Just about you and your God damn boundaries.

This was written at the same time as the poem above but not sent … just expressing my feelings…my anger. Later read it to E, crying as usual.

I am sad you don't care - didn't care - it was a business relationship. You provided a "service" - I paid for your time. But business relationships aren't intimate - delving into a person's most personal innermost thoughts and fantasies - anxieties and perceptions - love and hate - insecurities and imperfections.   It would have been better if you didn't write back. I'd have thought you were just applying those boundaries, but maybe you did actually care.

After reading that e-mail the one and only time, I was nauseous and so sad. I can't reread it again. **It's been a privilege working with you.** *Something you'd say to a contractor after he built your home or a committee member planning a PTA Fair. Not to someone you know better than anyone else on earth. Is that any way to treat a child - an inferior - a "less than" you? You and your profession made me this way - so deep into a therapeutic alliance I couldn't end it. You kept me in this turmoil - left me in distress and hurting. Just as much as you help people, you hurt them. And then go home and sleep like a baby. Your profession allows - advocates - is based on subordination and submission. You expect - no - demand - this inferior status. You're protected…I'm rejected. You're superior because your profession dictates I must be inferior to get better. You are apparently perfect…I have never even been close. You're on a pedestal…I'm on the ground looking up.*

I've lost my self respect for God's sakes. I grovel. I'd have even taken "the scraps from your table". (Loved that analogy).   What other profession would have this power to lessen a person. Build us up? No. We must be less than equal - a nobody - a nobody special. Good job. I asked for so little - even that was too much, wasn't it?

She came to him that first day
Quiet and sad.
Her feelings repressed.
She'd lost her Dad.
Time went on
Most things got better
Occasionally she wanted to give up
But he wouldn't let her.
All those years she felt loved and protected
Never criticized nor rejected
After 7 years he would walk away
Without a backward glance.
She begged him please give me just one more "dance"
But he flipped her off - shot her down - bid her adieu
Said it was a privilege working with you.
That was the sign
It was abundantly clear.
She understood now
He never ever cared. (or could be: It always was just a one-sided
love affair.)

****

In every life, tears must fall.
She'd had her share - she shed them all.
Outside her home she seemed emboldened.
Behind closed doors, her eyes were swollen.
She cried for him - it never stopped.
She never let go - she never forgot.
She missed him so - she ached to see him.
Alas her fantasies remained forbidden.
She asked herself: Will it ever end?
Will I ever stop loving my 50 minute friend?

****

She loved him more than Life itself.
She gave of her love - she gave of herself.
He went away - she was alone.
She felt like a child without a home.
She shuttered with excitement.
She trembled with desire.
She awoke from the dream.
Her thoughts were on fire.
She'd tried to move on
But her anchor was gone.
Trying to imagine Life without Him
Would be too hard - it would be too grim.
So She carefully counted out the pills - more than 105.
She took the leap
She closed her eyes
She fell back to sleep.
As the darkness fell, She drifted quietly into a final slumber.
Life was no longer worth living. .she realized she'd always been just a number.
So she ended it once and for all, that October morning in the Fall.

****

The tears I cry are for me…not you.
I understand now…after all I've been through.
You moved on…I couldn't … or wouldn't.
I still keep loving you…I know I shouldn't.
I've got to go on…be brave and be strong…for me.
But for awhile longer, I'll mourn
For the way it used to be.

****

I've come a long ways.
I've got further to go.
Would have been nice to keep taking it slow.
Wish You had continued the journey with me.
But alas, I it wasn't meant to be.

Wish you were here to see me grow.
I've worked so hard.
But you'll never know .
So sad and so needy just like a little kid.
Guess you don't care . Guess you never did.
(or: Too bad you don't care. Too bad you never did.)
****

She laid down on the hill in a shady place
She looked up at the clouds
As past her they raced
The sun so soft and so warm
Upon her face
She looked up again and felt God's grace.
The clouds moved slower now
Changing shapes
One in particular looked like his face
(or: She looked up again and imagined his face)
Excitedly she watched it's slow and steady pace
Till suddenly it was gone
His face was erased.
She got up and walked from the grassy knoll
Sadly again alone on her stroll.
She missed him more than words can say
She missed him more than yesterday.
Sadly she made her way through the flowers and clover
She was ready now - her life would soon be over.
Someone she loved had gone away
She was so angry he wouldn't stay
But he was no different than all the rest
He abandoned her, so alone she was left.
****

Loss like a family member but it's only MY loss - he's alive - he didn't die - he's just lost - he's gone - on to others who need him more- but I need Him - maybe they need him more...maybe.

He gave me his time - his faith - his presence - his SELF - I'll never forget what others have yet to experience - to appreciate.

The progression of grief ... my pathway of loss ... uneven, rocky, filled with obstacles...demons at every turn - they must be stopped - walked over - worked through - destroyed. Or I will be.

****

My mind pounds like the ocean's surf...
The thoughts rush in and then disperse.
Never silent, never still
They challenge me... they always will.
Decades filled with turmoil and strife
Seven years of counsel and advice.
Of course peace and serenity came with a price
But finally now I have back my life

****

Loved him more than life itself
Then suddenly he was gone... I was by myself.
Now when things get tough I am alone
No one can help me...
Have to do it on my own.
Didn't know what to feel
When all around me seemed unreal.
But I had to do it...I had no choice.
I had to learn to silence my voice.
No one left to listen... no one left to care
No one left to help from that faraway chair.
No one left to talk to... no one with whom to share
No one left to admire anywhere.
It's over now... he had to go.
Now no one will listen...no one will know.
Who's left to listen...with whom can I share?
I wonder often why isn't Life fair?
I told him "Don't linger...If you must leave, just go
But never forget I loved you so.

Sadly that was our last goodbye.
Loving Him was such a joy..
That October morning was our last "How have you been?"
I felt so badly it had to end.
Always a boundary - never a touch
Still I miss him so very much.
I'll go on. I'll be okay.
There'll just be a new normal
 Each and every day.
Things will never be the same
But I'll go on...it's all part of the game.
****

I Remind Myself You Are Gone...
The World as I Know It Must Go On.
Therefore I Must Close This Chapter of My Book...
Venturing Forward Without a Backwards Look.
I Wonder If You Know How Much I Love You Still.
I Wonder If You Know, I Always, Always Will.
I Wonder If You Knew How Much I Truly Cared...
And How Your Leaving Left Me Totally Unprepared.
The Pain Is Gone - The Love Remains...
Please Never Ever Let That Change.
I Miss Your Face, Your Voice, Your Smile Too...
But What I Really Miss is You.
****

From the depths of my heart (soul) I'm bleeding (hurting)
 Sadness and tears trickle forth (pour out)
The pain's (intense) not lessening;- it's taking my breath away -the
disease's cure is naught (is nowhere to be found)
The doctor's prognosis is poor - nothing to look forward to
Only the bleakness of time -- Alone -- without You
****

Hate Me...Hate You.
I'm so tired , I'm so sad.
Not to mention, Miss you Bad.

****

I lie here quietly trying to sleep
Instead I weep silently on the soft satin sheets.
The moon sat in the sky so high
Now it's disappearing as the dawn is nigh.
I try to remember your face
My memory dims and it's quickly erased.
I remember that tender feeling though
How I wish it was still so.
The light went out - the darkness came -
It helped not at all the intense pain -
I went to bed - I didn't sleep
No pray the Lord my soul to keep
When morning dawned I only prayed there'd be an end
To the love I felt for my Special Friend.

****

The following were the two poems I sent him that day when I requested an appointment. I think they show how much I truly appreciate and love him for all he has done for me.

I explored the depths of the unknown. Because of You.
I look to the Future and less to the Past. Because of You.
I felt the fear, but I did it anyway. Because of You.
I broke free of the pain. Because of You.
I loved completely. Because of You.
I grieved intensely. Because of You.
My world fell apart but I put it back together. Because of You.
I believe in Me. Because of You.
I'm letting go and moving on. Because of You.
I'll never forget being safe and protected...being heard and connected...all because of You.

How I wish that You could see
What a difference You made in Me.
I see the world through different eyes
All because of You and I.
I see the difference, I know it's true
All because of Me and You.
It's really real, it's really true
This Change all happened
Because of You.
Dr. Seuss I'll never be
But I'm still proud of what I see.
I've worked hard... I think it shows.
Everyday I feel I grow.
Thank you's not enough to say (though it will have to do.)
I'm in a better place today... all because of You.
I understand that time can heal
Though it can't change the way I feel.
I go on but I can't rest
All because I've known the Best.
Such an amazing man... don't you forget it.
Because of you, the sky's the limit.
Still some days I miss you so...
I guess I thought that You should know.
But most days my course is straight and even
All because of Dr. D-----s S------s!

My last (unsent) shortened letter on the subject of "rejection".

Well, here I am "talking" to you once again.

I really, really hurt when I got your rejection letter. I should have had low expectations. You always told me lower my expectations. And you'd certainly "shot me down" many times before. Why did I believe things would be different this time?   Deep down I thought you would want to see me and wondered how I was doing and would allow me the "closure" I never found that last day. It all went so fast. I didn't even really hug you. Don't even remember what it felt like - too rushed - too much emotion. (You know I'm mindless, right?) I had waited so long, and it meant - felt like - nothing.

I didn't shoot back an e-mail to you, did I, after you sent me the Rejection Letter (we will call it that for lack of a better word, ok?). That would not have been the case 8 years ago, would it? I wanted to say "That's your opinion" or "Screw You" or "You're Wrong" , but I didn't. I guess I had lost all my self worth by that time - there was nothing left. But surprisingly, even to me, I turned to painting and the angry, harsh strokes and dark colors that covered the canvas changed to soft, comforting colors and gentle strokes, and I relaxed. I don't paint well, but I enjoy what I create. I don't do what everybody else does. Remember that phrase? It applies to so many things in my life, doesn't it?

Funny, had you not "rejected" me, I might very well have not made an appointment anyway.   But it would have been MY choice, something I never was allowed to have in our "relationship" (or lack thereof).   I was scared and kinda embarrassed to see you again cause of my graphic upcoming novel (I think I will name it Unnecessary Boundaries).   I wondered if it would be "funny" between us because of the sexual content of some of The Book, so maybe I wouldn't have come to see you, but at least I would have known I had a choice, and you would have liked to see me if I did. I would have known if I needed you, you were still there.   You wouldn't let me down. You had to "move on" but you didn't totally abandon me. You still cared a little. If I had come, would you have made mean comments so as to make sure I never contacted you again? That would have devastated me. You wouldn't have done that. Would you?

I had wanted to ask these questions to you:

What is normal?

The book said therapists know things about you, even you don't know. What did you know about me?

Why weren't you comfortable with me taping the last appointment?

Why did you become a therapist? Did you give up being a minister because you'd have had to work weekends and wouldn't make much money? Just wondering...

Why couldn't you say something simple like "I'll miss our time together." Is it because you don't and knew you wouldn't?

Did you mind The Book and the main character's similarities to you? The references to people, places and things only you would understand? Were you angry at me for what I wrote? I'm sorry if that was the case. It really was a very special compilation. If you even read it, I hope you understand that.

Was I just a time slot? An insurance co-pay? I expect that's probably true, huh?

I wanted your approval sooo much. Why didn't you ever praise me? Why didn't you ever say anything kind, as a friend, rather than clinical and generic - textbook - all the way. Was it always just "cookie cutter" therapy? Just like reading a cookbook and following step by step directions. What to say and how to respond no matter what I told you. It would have meant more from you than any other person in the world to hear I did well. Didn't you know that? Or was there nothing to praise? Maybe that was the case.

I'll see you again sometime you know.   You probably won't see me…but I'll be there.   Because what you resist, persists.   Hi, my name is J.   I'm an addict.   I'm addicted to you.   The same as a cocaine addict.   You are my drug of choice as I said.   You were my "fix".   You soothed me…you made me feel good about myself and my life…you gave me a "high" each time I saw you.   Knowing you was such a pleasure…you certainly were a special treasure.

Do you think I will get over you?   I don't know what else to do, but love you and miss you.   I don't have anyone or anything to replace you with.   I so miss the relationship - the connection - if only for 50 minutes.

Though these past 8 months sucked, I was the luckiest person on earth to have been allowed to come to you - to be with the greatest man I know - to have the smartest and funniest "50 minute friend".   Your sense of humor was awesome.   You just came out with the most comical observations.   Each time I listen to the tape recordings, I appreciate the hours you spent with me.   I don't know where I would have been were it not for your advice and counsel over the years.   I talked - you listened - things did indeed get better.

JUNE 2014

There has been much time to think- to analyze my thoughts and feelings. I still go to the counseling center, but now it's for Grief Counseling. Being there evokes strong emotions in me. There's no doubt I feel D's presence there when I visit E for my appointments, but that's not necessarily a bad thing. We all grieve in our own way.

One day I sat looking out the window waiting for my appointment to begin, and I wrote the following essay. In writing it, I truly understood much of the reason for my need to be there. It wasn't just about the therapy. It was my safe place - my happy place - the best part of my life. There I was accepted. There I was protected. There I was Home. The following will explain how much this Center means to me:

Bursting through the heavy doors, anticipation in every step, she turns right, not the always certain left she had taken for more than seven years. She slowly makes her way down the familiar hallway. She is comfortable now peering into those open doors -those offices - those rooms she never knew existed at this opposite end of the corridor. His office that had permeated her thoughts - that intrigued her - that cast a mystique for so many years is smaller than she envisioned it would be. She imagined it would be large and filled with books and artifacts and the work of New England artists. She expected it would be massive - an office made for a man of his superior stature. Now, without his presence, it was simple - certainly not imposing - a room that could be used as another therapy room - not as a domain for a man of so many talents - so many titles - not an office to be occupied by an Executive Director. She, aware of the strict boundaries, never asked to step into his "kingdom" - to invade his private sanctum - not even once. She, therefore, envisioned it to be awesome - imposing - a "Palace" for the "King" whose personality it reflected.

It is quiet now. Few clients are there this early morning hour. Alone in the waiting room, just as during the car ride in this day, she begins to cry softly. It is unexpected - unexplainable - unfathomable after all these years.

Sitting there gazing out the window, watching the grey squirrel busily digging for long-lost nuts hidden under the dampened leaves, an awareness of why entering this building impacts her emotions to such an extent becomes evident. It is an "ah hah" moment. It is, she thinks, so obvious, yet it was so oblivious to her these many months and years.

It never was just about Him - just the appointments - the feelings - the emotions - the sharing. Just as he took the place of what was missing in her Life - a parent, lover, teacher, friend, confidant, soul mate and so much more - this building, too, became a missing part of her Life. Blindsided by the thought, she realizes...it is HOME.

Years before her childhood home had been demolished to make way for a neighbor's new modern dwelling. Her home for nearly 20 years - the home she lived in through her high school and college years - the one she returned to visit after she had moved away and which she would return to with her children when she and her former husband moved back to the area - where two of her children visited with Grandma and Grandpa when they were young - the home where she found solace when her first marriage fell apart - where her parents welcomed her whenever she came up the basement stairs - that too had been sold many years ago. It now stands hidden by tall trees and undergrowth, barely visible from the highway below. And there was her parents' home of more than 25 years - the house next door - the home filled with children, *grandchildren, memories of holidays and get togethers, the house she could always see from her living room window - the house she could always step into and know she was loved and would be cared for. That house, too, was sold after her parents' deaths. A new couple own it now but they have no children, no noisy gatherings, no Easter egg hunts on the lawn, no horse rides in the driveway, no grandchildren waiting for the school bus on their first days of school and every day thereafter.*

She has her own house, of course, but the memories are not as poignant - not as comforting. The children for the most part have moved away - have moved on with their own lives. There is little love in the house now filled with arguments and disagreements, dislike, distain and disappointment except when the "loves of her life", the grandchildren make their visits.

But once every two weeks for all these years, she found her HOME - her sanctuary - her refuge - her serenity - her happy place - her calm - her caring - her foundation. And now pondering if she has become the guest who has overstayed her welcome, the tears, the loneliness, the emptiness return. Now she will be not only an adult orphan, but an adult homeless orphan and her inner child cries out for the loss. Like an uprooted tree, her roots - her soul - lie exposed and barren. No one - nothing to hold her up - to support her - to keep her from bending - to keep her from breaking and falling into the dark abyss. She is once again inconsolable. Loss continues to impact and invade her life. And she continues to grieve for what was and will never be again.

AFTERTHOUGHTS

And so, therapy draws to an end. The prognosis is good. The post therapy period is nearly over. I am no longer a "child" nor a "childlike adult" but an adult in every sense of the word. I do see more clearly now. It's easier to put my life - my therapy - my grieving - in perspective. "When you know better, you do better". Maya Angelou was right.

I learned so many things from D. He gave me tools to live my life. He urged me, first and foremost, to set boundaries and say No when I just didn't want to do something (for others). His advice resonates each and every day. "Think what you would do if you were alone and do it". "Lower your expectations" (about so many different people and things). "People in nursing homes have all the time in the world and wish they didn't" (addressed to the complaint while I worked that I had no time). "In your defense, you have emotional disturbances but you're working through them." "Anxieties are not necessarily caused by childhood experiences, but by chemical imbalances". "Simplify". "Don't take everything personally". "If you put something up in the garage out of sight, then it's not readily available, so why keep it?" (and so I got rid of hundreds of cookbooks I never read or used). (When agonizing about disposing of things left from my parents' estate) "Did they tell you that you had to keep those things?" (Of course not) "What would be gained by it?" (when considering confronting someone or doing something I wasn't sure of). "A week has 168 hours and you only have to spend 40 of them with the people at work". He showed me situations need not be fearful. I could conquer the fear and it would dissipate. (On not liking myself) "Why don't you? Everybody else does. Are they all wrong?"

Because of transference and an ironclad therapeutic alliance, D became everything to me. A parent, a counselor, a teacher, a minister, a lover (emotionally not physically) and a 50 minute friend. He was my "Rock". I'm trying to learn to accept what is and what possibly will never be again. To this day, I would love to just talk to him one more time. I would hope that as time has passed, I would have matured and my perception of him, in another setting, knowing he had new clients and I wasn't one of them, would have lessened the craving, the yearning, the desire I have for him. I just want to know he's okay. I need closure. I want my life back. I want to live again. Please.

Now back on a small dosage of mood stabilizing medication, I can reflect on how grateful I am to this man who entered my life at its lowest point, and taught me to live and love again. It was my privilege and pleasure to have spent probably 200 hours with him over a 7 plus year period. He was the most intelligent, most educated, most respected and admired man I've ever known. He was honest and dependable and funny and never critical and demeaning. He was "there" for me, just me. He was "present". He was sophisticated and classy and so far "out of my league", we weren't even in "the same ballpark"... yet so down- to- earth and compassionate. He was tall and handsome and showed me a man over 60 could be active and full of life. I marvel at how lucky I was to have known him, to have spent time with him, and to have been counseled by him. He was an Executive Director, a minister, a therapist, a Doctor of Education, a nephew of a famous writer, an author, adjunct faculty and supervisor of young therapists for numerous colleges, yet he had the time to see ME every two weeks for more than 7 years. How lucky could a person get, right? Thank goodness he agreed to meet with me that first day. I shudder to think what would have occurred over these past 8 years if he had not.

And most importantly, my confidence and self esteem grew immeasurably over those years together. He encouraged me to follow my passion wherever it took me. Thus, not only did I retire and write this book, but I also have a romantic novel which will be coming out in a few months. I believe all therapy patients - former, present and future - will enjoy this upcoming book, based on a main character much like D and a patient (remarkably like the author) years later, at a different point in their lives, and the romance that develops due to unexpected circumstances, where boundaries are unnecessary and love flourishes - if only for one year. I gave D a copy before he moved. It would have meant the world to me to know for certain that he at least took the time to read it and understood it is a very special 2 year long project written especially for him…and me.

Researching transference, I found a wonderful blog (dearzanny.com) by Suzanne Maiden. The particular topic was "5 Things Your Therapist is Really Thinking". I want to believe that deep down, D feels the same way about his clients, including me. She writes:

"… as a therapist, I grow to love my clients. I mean I really, really, love my clients with such a tenderness I get chills thinking about it. No matter how kooky (that should be a clinical term), no matter how warped, no matter how ill they may be--I love them. I realize their inner turmoil and current level of functioning is a direct result of their woundedness. As C.G. Jung asked, "How is the symptom serving the soul?" He meant how are people's neurosis their method of "fixing" what's broken. It may appear dysfunctional by others' standards, but to know all is to understand all. It all makes sense if you discard logic. I get the honor of sitting with them as they process their deepest woundings. I get the privilege of hearing their deepest secrets. I am often the first person with whom they share their most inner world. The phrase that speaks to this so well, is Carl Rogers' concept of 'Unconditional Positive Regard' for the client. I resonate with the Rogerian approach. I see my clients' psychological warts and wrinkles, and they are still beautiful to me. This is what I think as a therapist. This is my therapeutic stance. Because no matter how brilliant my interpretations and predictions are, if my client does not experience a therapeutic lovingness from me, they will not permanently heal to their fullest capacity."

Although D never opened up and shared any feelings with me, I hope his therapeutic stance mirrors Suzanne's, because if it does, then the answer to my question "Did he care?" will be answered. Unless he feels comfortable contacting me,(and , of course, I hope after reading this, he might), I'll never know one way or the other...but I choose to believe in his own way, maybe he cared for me...for all his clients.

My fervent hope is by opening up my Life and my grief to the general public, individuals will learn therapy from the "inside out" and thus, in some small way, I can make a difference in their lives as D did in mine. Agreeing to that first appointment with D 8 years ago was the best life-changing decision I've ever made. It is the only decision I have made in my life that was carried out with complete confidence and for which I have absolutely no regrets.

Thank you, D. Without you, this book, poems, song lyrics and the novel to follow, would never have come to fruition. You have been my guiding light. You spark in me creativity and passion. I would not be the person I have become if it were not for you. **I could not have wished for a better outcome.**

Oh, and one last thing. Please come home...you've been gone long enough.

"

**MY RIGHT HAND POINTING TO LANDSCAPES OF CONTINENTS AND THE PUBLIC ROAD...
NOT I, NOT ANYONE ELSE CAN TRAVEL THAT ROAD FOR YOU, YOU MUST TRAVEL IT FOR YOURSELF**

WALT WHITMAN, "A SONG OF MYSELF"

ABOUT THE AUTHOR

Born in a small village in Upstate New York on the 4th of July, 1950, the author has spent most of her life in Northern New York, except for brief stops in Providence, Rhode Island, where she graduated from Johnson and Wales Junior College of Business with a degree in Court Reporting, and in Boston, Massachusetts, New Haven, Connecticut and Newport, Rhode Island, where she lived while working as a legal secretary.

Now retired and the grandmother of 8, including a set of twin boys, she is pursuing the passion that was smothered and forgotten during those years raising 4 children, taking care of aging parents and continuing a boring, but secure, career in the oil industry. She is now enjoying her freedom and the opportunity to finally partake in many interests and activities, most especially writing this book, as well as a romantic fantasy novel soon to be published .

THE END